Crosscurrents / MODERN CRITIQUES
NEW SERIES

George J. Searles

The Fiction of
PHILIP ROTH and
JOHN UPDIKE

Southern Illinois University Press
CARBONDALE AND EDWARDSVILLE

Printed in the United States of America
Edited by Kevin B. Goulding
Designed by Bob Nance
Production supervised by Kathleen Giencke

Permission to quote from the following sources is gratefully acknowledged:

Alfred A. Knopf, Inc., for excerpts from works by John Updike: *Assorted Prose*, 1965; *Bech: A Book*, 1970; *Bech is Back*, 1982; *The Centaur*, 1963; *Couples*, 1968; *A Month of Sundays*, 1975; *Of the Farm*, 1965; *Picked Up Pieces*, 1976; *Pigeon Feathers*, 1962; *The Poorhouse Fair*, 1982; *Rabbit Is Rich*, 1981; *Rabbit Redux*, 1971; *Rabbit Run*, 1960; *The Same Door*, 1972; *Telephone Poles and Other Poems*, 1963; and *Tossing and Turning*, 1977.

Jonathan Cape Ltd. for excerpts from works by Philip Roth: *The Professor of Desire*, *Reading Myself and Others*, and *Zuckerman Unbound*.

Andre Deutsch for excerpts from works by John Updike: *Rabbit Is Rich*, 1981; and *Rabbit Redux*, 1960.

Random House for excerpts from works by Philip Roth: *Letting Go*, 1962; and *Portnoy's Complaint*, 1969.

from *Goodbye, Columbus* by Philip Roth. Copyright © 1959 by Philip Roth. Reprinted by permission of Houghton Mifflin Company

excerpts from *Zuckerman Unbound* copyright © 1981 by Philip Roth, excerpts from *Reading Myself and Others* copyright © 1961, 1963, 1969, 1970, 1971, 1972, 1973, 1974, 1975 by Philip Roth, and excerpts from *The Professor of Desire* copyright © 1977 by Philip Roth. Reprinted by permission of Farrar, Strauss, & Giroux, Inc.

Library of Congress Cataloging in Publication Data

Searles, George J. (George John), 1944-
    The fiction of Philip Roth and John Updike.
    (Crosscurrents/Modern critiques/new series)
    Bibliography: p.
    Includes index.
    1. American fiction—20th century—History and criticism. 2. Roth, Philip —Criticism and interpretation. 3. Updike, John—Criticism and interpretation. I. Title. II. Series: Crosscurrents/modern critiques. New series.
PS379.S398   1985   813'.54'09   84-1269
ISBN 0-8093-1175-5

to Ellis

Contents

Acknowledgements

For granting permission to quote from Philip Roth's and John Updike's books, the authors' publishers are hereby gratefully acknowledged: Andre Deutsch, Ltd.; Farrar, Strauss & Giroux, Inc.; Houghton Mifflin Co.; Jonathan Cape, Ltd.; and Random House, Inc./Alfred A. Knopf, Inc.

And I wish also to thank those individuals who in various other ways have helped me to complete this volume: Ms. Barbara Granato of the Mohawk Valley Community College Biology Department, who typed the manuscript; Professor Eugene Paul Nassar of the Utica College English Department, who offered advice and guidance; President Sheldon N. Grebstein of the State University College at Purchase, New York, under whose tutelage the study first took shape; Mr. Frank Tedeschi, who shared my early enthusiasm for Roth and Updike, and remains my indispensable friend; my in-laws, Sidney and Irene Gage, for their ongoing encouragement and support; my mother, Mrs. Kathryn Searles, and my sons, Jonathan and Colin, for deepening my understanding of life and therefore of literature; and my wife, Ellis, for her editorial assistance and critical judgement, but more importantly for her love.

1

Roth and Updike:
Social Realists in an Unreal Society

IN A RICHLY INSIGHTFUL ESSAY entitled "Writing American Fiction," Philip Roth observed that "the American writer in the middle of the twentieth century has his hands full in trying to understand, describe, and then make *credible* much of American reality. It stupifies, it sickens, it infuriates, and finally it is even a kind of embarrassment to one's own meager imagination. The actuality is continually outdoing our talents, and the culture tosses up figures almost daily that are the envy of any novelist."[1] Although these remarks were first published in 1961, they are perhaps even more accurate today. The situation that Roth describes still exists and partly accounts for the recent proliferation of experimental novels that challenge all previous definitions of the genre. Daringly innovative and elaborately metaphorical, the books of writers such as Thomas Pynchon, William Gaddis, Robert Coover, and others have responded in ways increasingly bizarre and fantastical to an apparently untenable world, adopting surrealistic distortion as their mode. And in the process, they have greatly expanded our conception of what the novel can be.

At the same time, however, the realistic novel has continued to flourish. Like Saul Bellow and a number of others, Philip Roth himself is essentially a social realist, a novelist of manners. Although his career has encompassed some experimental ventures, in his best and most representative works he has created strikingly vivid impressions of American society today. John Updike is another who has warmly embraced the novelist's customary role of social historian and commentator. In his major novels and stories he has convincingly captured the collective American personality and the dilemmas with which it grapples. As one critic has succinctly put it, "Updike offers the novel's traditional pleasures."[2] Surely the same could be said of Roth.

In so fashioning their fictions, both Roth and Updike have naturally attracted a wide general readership; their books are assigned in college literature courses, but are also best sellers. This is important if we accept the Platonic conception of the artist as moral guardian of society. Although they are not (and may never be) "great" in the sense that Hawthorne and Melville, for example, are said to be, Roth and Updike are nevertheless highly skilled writers whose novels and stories richly repay close scrutiny. Accordingly, a number of books and a great many scholarly essays have been devoted to their work, but—perhaps because of their obvious differences— Roth and Updike have seldom been discussed in relation to each other. Such a joint consideration is overdue, as a comparative approach to these writers will yield fresh, interesting perspectives on both. This book uses just such a strategy to convey a fuller understanding of each writer's vision and to examine the techniques employed in bringing that vision to artistic fruition.

The two writers have a great deal in common. Some of these parallels are superficial, mere accidents of chronology, but others are quite substantial. Each published his first book of fiction (Roth's *Goodbye, Columbus* and Updike's *Poorhouse Fair*) in 1959. Both have won the National Book Award (Roth for *Goodbye, Columbus* and Updike for *The Centaur*) and numerous other literary prizes. They are but a year apart in age. Updike was born on March 18, 1932, Roth, on March 19, 1933. Thus, they have been shaped by a number of common influences and are writing in and about the same moment. Further, there is a shared geographical orientation; both are natives of the Northeast and locate the great majority of their fictions there. Both are recognized as highly individual stylists, adept at reinforcing the literal surfaces of their works with a skillfully symbolic underpinning. Through the filtering (and frequently distorted) perspective of suffering protagonists who are often thinly-veiled autobiographical projections, both writers address the same large social issues: ethnic identity, family relationships, individual moral responsibility and guilt, sexuality and romantic love, materialism, and social mores in general.

There are, of course, major divergences between them. Most fundamental is their differing ethnic backgrounds: Roth's Jewishness and Updike's W.A.S.P. identity. These dissimilar heritages have been instrumental not only in determining how the two authors treat their dominant thematic concerns, but also in influencing some of the technical aspects of their methodologies. This is noticeable, for example, in such areas as narrative perspective, setting, character types, and style.

As a Jewish-American artist, Roth evinces a prevailingly Jewish angle of perception. This is certainly not to suggest that he speaks for all Jewish Americans, or that his work con-

stitutes a manifesto. But his protagonists, his principally urban backdrops, his use of language, and his thematic emphases all reflect the Jewish-American experience. Among
Roth's central concerns, for example, is the ongoing problem
of cultural assimilation. Many of his protagonists struggle, in
varying degrees, with the psychological conflicts that this adjustment engenders. They are also city-dwellers, as is largely
true of the actual Jewish-American population, which has
tended to cluster in and around the urban centers. Similarly,
their language and that of their families and associates echoes
actual Jewish-American speech, by blending educated
American English, urban argot, and Yiddish-influenced dia-
lect patterns.

The most controversial feature of Roth's fiction has been
the ambivalence with which many of his characters perceive
their Jewishness. They seem to view themselves as at once
both enhanced and diminished by their heritage. In treating
this idea, Roth sometimes depicts a fundamental contrast between two opposed ways of life: the more traditional, Euro-
pean mode of Jewishness, and the secularized, "modern" existence embraced by the fully assimilated. Indeed, the
resulting tension is among Roth's most obvious concerns in
his earlier work, particularly in *Goodbye, Columbus* and *Portnoy's Complaint*. And even if it is not so apparent in his recent
books, it still functions there as a very real source of the com-
munications barrier between generations. In the "Zuckerman" novels, for example, the titular protagonist experiences great difficulty understanding—and being understood
by—his parents and other family members, largely because
of the differing world views embraced by Nathan and his
family.

If Roth's work is essentially Jewish, Updike repeatedly
writes of the embattled W.A.S.P., the threatened species

whose former cultural preeminence has been challenged—
and now practically attenuated—by inexorable social
change. Like Roth's protagonists, then, Updike's "heroes"
exist in a climate of adjustment, and in their own ways they
confront various identity crises. But Updike's larger, overriding theme is that of cultural disintegration, motivating such
diverse works as *The Poorhouse Fair*, *The Centaur*, *Couples*, *Problems*, and the "Rabbit" novels. Whether the protagonist is a
rural, urban, or suburban character, the crises he encounters
are invariably caused, at least in part, by a breakdown of the
established order. Thus, Updike addresses many of our most
pressing concerns: the lack of meaningful work, the dehu-
manization caused by over bureaucratization, the negative
effects of materialistic excess, the dissolution of marriage and
family life, and even—in *Rabbit Redux*—the conundrum of
race relations. Like Roth's, his perspective is that of one who
has seen better, and who pines for "the good old days" of a
simpler and presumably purer America. Just as Roth chides
his characters not for being Jewish, but for being not Jewish
enough, Updike's focus is traditionally Christian, a blending
of his childhood Lutheranism and the neoorthodox theology
of Karl Barth.

The two writers' very different religious-ethnic heritages
ultimately lead them to common ground. Each repeatedly
portrays questing, alienated protagonists whose personal
shortcomings are largely mitigated by the fact that these
characters function in a meretricious environment, a moral
wasteland unredeemed by the traditional pieties and received
wisdom that sustained earlier generations.

The most truly significant difference between Roth and
Updike is one of perspective. While Updike adopts a broad,
almost sociological approach, Roth tends toward a more in-
trospective handling of his material. His books are as much

character studies of the protagonists as they are commentaries on the current scene. Accordingly, Roth's works are almost always written in the first person ("spoken," as it were, by their protagonists), while Updike's are usually in the form of third person. Members of a mistreated minority, Roth's characters are more concerned with personal survival than with the larger society that has excluded them. But for Updike's W.A.S.P.'s, themselves integral components of the failed system, individual and society are more inextricably linked. In short, Roth's characters are in search of a sophisticated, existential self-knowledge that will enable them to function independently in a world where "the center cannot hold"; Updike's people seem to be seeking an external rationale for a traditional "leap of faith" that will somehow restore a sense of stability and Christian community to that world.

But this is not to say that Roth is concerned only with personality and Updike only with the social structure; such a suggestion would be far too reductive indeed. Surely, Roth's works all reveal a deep concern for the state of society, even while illustrating his claim that "when Edmund Wilson says that after reading *Life* magazine he feels he does not belong to the country depicted there, that he does not live in this country, I understand what he means."[3] From *Goodbye, Columbus* to Roth's latest books, the difficulties encountered by the Rothian protagonist are certainly not experienced in a vacuum and in fact are often exacerbated by what Roth terms the "struggle . . . going on today between self and culture."[4] The conclusion of *Zuckerman Unbound* reinforces this most dramatically, as Zuckerman surveys the blasted streets of a ruined Newark and tells himself, "you don't come from anywhere anymore."[5]

Similarly, Updike could hardly be accused of sacrificing character for theme. Except, perhaps, for Jerry Conant of

Marry Me, Updike's major characters are all fully rendered creations. Some are more successfully evoked than others, but all reveal their author's keen insight into human personality and psychology. Protagonists such as George Caldwell and Harry Angstrom (at each stage of his development) come immediately to mind as complex, entirely believable figures whose inner workings are finely delineated within the compass of Updike's broad social panorama.

In summary, Roth and Updike have demonstrated a comprehensive mastery of the novel's traditional virtues and each has contributed several decidedly superior works that are quite likely to endure. It is to Roth and Updike that future generations of literary critics and social demographers will most profitably return when seeking fictions from which to derive a felt sense of life in the troubled second half of the twentieth century. Accordingly, these writers' fictions warrant careful exploration even now, for therein we find mirrored our own foibles and frailties, as well as our enduring human capacity for survival and occasional transcendence.

To evaluate the two authors' achievement to date, this book concentrates on selected works by each and explores in successive chapters the central thematic preoccupations shared by Roth and Updike: ethnicity, family ties, romantic relationships, and several subsidiary themes. For the sake of compression, coherence, and literary discrimination, the discussion addresses their major novels, with allusions to short stories and secondary works where appropriate. In Roth's case, particular attention is paid to *Goodbye, Columbus, Letting Go, Portnoy's Complaint, The Professor of Desire,* and the "Zuckerman" novels. The treatment of Updike focuses principally on *Couples, The Centaur, Of the Farm,* and the "Rabbit" novels.

Of course, these works are assessed with regard not only to content, but also to form. Each writer's novels are closely analyzed, not simply as thesis statements, but as *belles lettres;* particular attention is given—throughout the book and in detail in a separate chapter—to considerations of literary technique, touching upon such matters as narrative perspective, setting, language, and symbolism. And an entire chapter is devoted to the writers' experimental works. The conclusion briefly traces the artistic evolution of both writers, and it attempts to assess their current status and to suggest some possible future developments in their unfolding careers.

2

"Roots": Ethnic/Cultural Background in Roth and Updike

THE DEDICATION PAGE of critic Sanford Pinsker's monograph on Philip Roth reads, "For my Mother, who hoped I would write about somebody else."[1] Pinsker's quip is immediately understood by anyone familiar with Roth's oeuvre, a body of fiction that has engendered great resentment in the Jewish community. Roth has been accused of creating distorted and demeaning portrayals of the Jewish-American experience, and his work has also been assailed as tasteless and obscene. Ironically, two of his most accomplished books, *Goodbye, Columbus* and *Portnoy's Complaint*, have elicited the most hostile responses.

Roth has repeatedly asserted, however, that he views himself as neither a spokesperson nor an apologist for American Jews, but as an artist. As early as 1963, he published in *Commentary* an impeccably well-reasoned and often cuttingly humorous essay, "Writing About Jews," in response to the numerous charges already lodged against him. In effect a position paper, the piece is a model of incisive counterattack. Roth argues throughout that any attempt on his part to depict only the positive aspects of his subject would in fact constitute a disservice to it. He recapitulates his statements made at an earlier symposium in Israel: "it is really a matter of who, in addressing them [the Jews], is going to take them more seriously . . . who is going to see them as something more than . . . helpless and threatened and in need of reassurance that they are as 'balanced' as anyone else. The question really is, who is going to address men and women like men and women, and who like children."[2]

Nevertheless, the widespread resistance to Roth's work is not surprising. Repeatedly, he depicts unattractive characters and situations, and the fact that his protagonists and settings are almost always Jewish has consequently created understandably mixed feelings among many readers. *Goodbye, Columbus,* for example, is a book in which no one fares particularly well. The "old world" Newarkers—represented by Aunt Gladys, a stock figure reminiscent of Malamud's Ida Bober in *The Assistant*—are ludicrous stereotypes; the prosperous suburban Patimkins are presented as crassly materialistic. Cultural disparity provides dramatic tension, but protagonist Neil Klugman is "a man without a country," evincing considerable distaste toward both the city environment and the world of suburban affluence. Although he ridicules Aunt Gladys, he shares her misgivings about the "new Jews," and seizes every opportunity to describe them in unflattering terms. He sees his own background as too limited and confining, but he believes that among recently assimilated suburban Jews, family warmth and selfless concern have been replaced by a shallow, *arriviste* value system that breeds dissension, insincerity, and calculating self-interest.

The short story "Eli, the Fanatic" makes essentially the same allegations, while Roth's first full-length novel, *Letting Go,* features a young protagonist who adopts an archly condescending posture of aloof disapproval toward the other characters, many of whom are Jewish. In the later short story "On the Air," Jewish elements function (as in "Epstein" and *The Great American Novel*) in a context of comic exaggeration. *My Life as a Man* concerns Peter Tarnopol, another Jewish protagonist whose situation is no less unsavory. And in the "Zuckerman" novels the volatile questions raised in "Writing About Jews" are again considered as the author Nathan Zuckerman clashes with various family members who have been angered by his portrayals of Jewish life. There is much autobiography in these recent books, as if Roth were again settling personal scores.

In any case, however, *Portnoy's Complaint* (like Zuckerman's *Carnofsky*) remains Roth's most controversial novel. Not mysteriously, it is the book most often cited when charges of anti-Semitism are brought against Roth. A compulsive masturbator and chronic whiner, Portnoy attributes the bulk of his difficulties to his background, and much of the novel consists of crude, slapstick versions of the Jewish experience. In addition, the book is unabashedly prurient, chronicling in explicit detail and uninhibited language the orgastic exploits of the protagonist, whose problems are summarized in the ersatz encyclopedia entry that prefaces the narrative:

Portnoy's Complaint (pôrt-noiz kəm-plānt) n. [after Alexander Portnoy (1933–)] A disorder in which strongly-felt ethical and altruistic impulses are perpetually warring with extreme sexual longings, often of a perverse nature. Spielvogel says: 'Acts of exhibitionism, voyeurism, fetishism, auto-eroticism and oral coitus are plentiful; as a consequence of the patient's "morality," however, neither fantasy nor act issues in genuine sexual gratification, but rather in overriding feelings of shame and the dread of retribution, particularly in the form of castration.' (Spielvogel, O. "The Puzzled Penis," *Internationale Zeitschrift für Psychoanalyse,* Vol. XXIV p.

909.) It is believed by Spielvogel that many of the symptoms can be traced to the bonds obtaining in the mother-child relationship.[3]

On the most obvious level, this fictionalized documentation presages the basically slapstick, farcical tone of what is to follow. Secondly, it signals the essentially profane nature of the book's content. Perhaps most importantly, however, it reveals that beneath the surface of this extremely humorous work are concerns of a very serious nature. For all its hilariously irreverent comedy, the novel is presented as the record of a psychological "complaint." The narrative is a disjointed, stream-of-consciousness monologue delivered by analysand Portnoy on the couch of his listening psychiatrist, Dr. Spielvogel.

But the encyclopedia definition makes no reference to the fact that Portnoy blames his problems on his Jewishness and believes that he will achieve stability only by renouncing that heritage. He sees the Jewish cultural ethos as productive only of repression and neurotic self-abasement. That the ethnic factor is at the very heart of the book is reinforced by Roth's comments in an *American Poetry Review* article revealing the genesis of Alexander Portnoy. He explains that the novel was inspired by his Jewish students at the Iowa Writers Workshop. The recurring figure in their short stories was the stereotypically overprotected adolescent son.[4] From there it was but a short step to selecting the psychoanalytic setting, a device he had already experimented with in an *Esquire* short story, "The Psychoanalytic Special." This framework enabled him to create a narrative voice that "could speak in behalf of both 'the Jewboy' (with all that word signifies to Jew and Gentile alike about aggression, appetite, and marginality) and the 'nice Jewish boy' (and what that epithet implies about repression, respectability, and social acceptance)."[5]

Clearly, then, *Portnoy's Complaint* depends for its very existence upon its author's perceptions of ethnicity.

There are, however, significant differences between
Roth's novel and the tradition of self-deprecating Jewish humor from which it derives. Irving Howe has pointed out, for
example, that after World War II, when Jewish humor began
to take on an abrasive, self-lacerating quality, there remained
an element of nostalgia, a shared sense of relief between per-
former and audience that it was "no longer necessary to be
careful. . . . no longer necessary to be defensive." Even in
the 1960s, when Jewish humor began to manifest a more obvious air of self-directed malice, much of the self-contempt
was the product of embarrassment "not so much about the
culture from which they had emerged (or, as some felt, escaped) but about the shame they could still feel at their own
ethnic denials and evasions. . . . Jewish entertainers moved
. . . toward a rasping aggressiveness, an arrogant declara-
tion of a despised Jewishness."[6] Obviously, then, there was
in the self-criticism of these performers—even in that of the
scathing Lenny Bruce—a coterminous current of ethnic
pride.

In *Portnoy's Complaint*, however, the protagonist's ravings
are for the most part entirely denunciatory of his heritage.
And there are indications that Portnoy is to some extent a
persona of Roth, that his strident denunciations constitute
(albeit in exaggerated form) a fictive expression of the author's feelings. Nevertheless, it would be mistaken to interpret Portnoy's diatribes as totally reflective of Roth's attitudes, for he obviously intends Portnoy as a portrayal of an
extremely unstable individual. Portnoy envisions himself as
a typical Jewish male and repeatedly phrases his grievances
in the first person plural, as in this passage: "Doctor Spielvogel, this is my life, my only life, and I'm living it in the mid-

dle of a Jewish joke! I am the son in the Jewish joke—*only it ain't no joke!* Please, who crippled us like this? Who made us so morbid and hysterical and weak?" (pp. 36–37). But Roth presents Portnoy neither as a representative Jew, nor as a representative man.

Rather, Portnoy emerges not only as an uncommonly intelligent, perceptive, and accomplished individual (he is New York City's Assistant Human Opportunity Commissioner under Mayor Lindsay), but as uncommonly callous, self-obsessed, and disturbed, as well. Further, it is the sheer excessiveness of his situation—most obviously exemplified by his prodigious feats of masturbation—that makes his story worthy of book-length presentation. In short, he is hardly the sort of character that Roth would be likely to choose as a self-projection. Roth has addressed this matter on several occasions, dismissing as naïve and simplistic the too-common practice of equating characters with their authors. The success of *Portnoy's Complaint* partially resulted from such misconstruction, and Roth has correctly theorized that his somewhat rakish image is "a concoction spawned by *Portnoy's Complaint* and compounded largely out of the fantasies that book gave rise to because of its 'confessional' strategy."[7]

It should be obvious that Alexander Portnoy is intended as a tragic figure; by the end of the novel he is thoroughly confused and desperate for any assistance that Spielvogel might be able to provide. He is, in sum, a very different person from the composed, self-assured, painstakingly rational individual who emerges in Roth's interviews and essays. Perhaps the temptation to view Portnoy as an authorial projection arises from a tendency to respond to the novel solely on the basis of its surface attractions: its antic humor, its witty irreverence, and its seemingly "liberated" sexual candor. Despite his manic insouciance, however, Portnoy is a broken man.

As Roth has told Joyce Carol Oates, "Sheer Playfulness and Deadly Seriousness are my closest friends,"[8] and the frolicsomely ribald surface of *Portnoy's Complaint* represents but one level of the book's total meaning.

Portnoy's psychological response to sexuality, and his correspondingly distorted dealings with women, illustrate most revealingly his basic inability to transcend the crippling limitations of an overriding self-centeredness. In each of his affairs, Portnoy exploits the woman. Even his habit of assigning depersonalizing titles to his lovers reveals that he views them not as individual human beings but simply as objects. Kay Campbell, Portnoy's college heartthrob, is called "The Pumpkin" not only because of her rotundity, but because to Portnoy she represents rural America, the agrarian Midwest. Portnoy is fascinated by the gentile ambience of her home when he visits for the Thanksgiving holiday, and initially feels that the W.A.S.P. lifestyle is superior to his own. But the relationship disintegrates after she dismisses Portnoy's suggestion that she convert to Judaism. That such an idea occurs to him so naturally reveals his basic confusion. He is at first attracted to Kay because she is not Jewish, but he ultimately rejects her for the same reason. This establishes a pattern that will remain constant in his other affairs, as well.

Portnoy's adult relationship with the patrician Sarah Abbot Maulsby, a New Canaan–Foxcroft–Vassar alumna whom he calls "The Pilgrim," is finally written off as "just something nice a son once did for his dad. A little vengeance on Mr. Lindabury for all those nights and Sundays Jack Portnoy spent collecting down in the colored district. A little bonus extracted from Boston & Northeastern, for all those years of service, and exploitation" (pp. 240–41). Again, what emerges is that Portnoy's desire for sexual conquest and his concomitant inability to love are linked to his Jewishness.

This aspect of Portnoy's situation is best illustrated by his tumultuous ten-month affair with Mary Jane Reed, whose wildly uninhibited sexual gusto earns her the appellation "The Monkey." The most fully-rendered of Portnoy's lovers, she is a New York fashion model who has risen from "poor white" origins to captivate the sophisticated Commissioner Portnoy. Despite her pose of mean-spirited rural ignorance, in reality she is a rather intelligent and sensitive person, and is attracted to Portnoy because she sees in him the opportunity for a significant relationship. Her appeal for Portnoy, however, lies solely in her unbridled lasciviousness. She is the living embodiment of his adolescent sexual fantasies, "Thereal McCoy" incarnate, someone with whom to act out his wildest imaginings.

But he is unable to find happiness even with this "girl of his (erotic) dreams," precisely because he suddenly finds himself growing fond of her. After their idyllic weekend in Vermont (strongly reminiscent of the pastoral Connecticut interlude in Nathanael West's *Miss Lonelyhearts*), during which the first stirrings of romantic love appear, Portnoy at once experiences doubts and misgivings. After they talk of love and Mary Jane rhapsodizes about marriage, Portnoy contrives to degrade the relationship in his own eyes. He induces Mary Jane to participate in a ménage à trois with him and a prostitute, and then dismisses the whole affair as simply another sexual fling, devoid of any true feeling or commitment.

To some extent, his problem can be seen as oedipal in nature. Sheldon Norman Grebstein has called the book "the most detailed account we have had of the tone and texture of the Jewish oedipal family experience."[9] Portnoy is fairly obviously the victim of his mother's inadvertently overzealous (and overseductive) affections. Consequently, he is unable to reconcile love and desire in later life because of his unconscious observance of the incest taboo. Like Updike's Harry

Angstrom, he cannot fuse *eros* and *agape*. Sex becomes in Portnoy's mind an evil and a means to subvert what he perceives as a too-restrictive ethical system inculcated during his upbringing. In his attempt to free himself from the demanding rigors of the role of "nice Jewish boy," he turns first to excessive masturbation. Indeed, the innumerable madcap scenes chronicling his prodigious feats in this area of activity (one entire chapter is entitled "WHACKING OFF") prompted one reviewer to term the novel "a sort of *Moby Dick* of masturbation."[10]

Unfortunately for Portnoy, however, adult sexuality becomes simply an extension of this childhood compulsion. His sexual affairs with women serve much the same purpose as does his masturbation, becoming little more than a means of defying what he sees as a too-restrictive cultural indoctrination. He tells Spielvogel that he wishes to "PUT THE ID BACK IN YID! Liberate this nice Jewish boy's libido" (p. 124), for he naively believes that reticence and repression are exclusively Jewish phenomena:

What else, I ask you, were all those prohibitive dietary rules and regulations all about to begin with, what else but to give us little Jewish children practice in being repressed? Practice, darling, practice, practice, practice. Inhibition doesn't grow on trees, you know—takes patience, takes concentration, takes a dedicated and self-sacrificing parent and a hard-working attentive little child to create in only a few years' time a really constrained and tight-ass human being. Why else the two sets of dishes? Why else the kosher soap and salt? Why else, I ask you, but to remind us three times a day that life is boundaries and restrictions if it's anything, hundreds of thousands of little rules laid down by none other than None Other (pp. 79–80).

Although Portnoy's desire to lead a more spontaneous, uninhibited life is a worthy goal, the obsessive single-mindedness with which he pursues sexual gratification as a means to that end renders his sex life ultimately unfulfilling and degraded. His objectification of his sex partners, further complicated by his oedipal confusions, results in neurosis.

Surely Portnoy's irrational behavior makes him an "unreliable narrator." Hence all of his actions and statements are open to debate, and his denunciations of his ethnic background are therefore suspect. As Patricia Meyer Spacks says in an excellent *Yale Review* essay, "Portnoy sees his own problems as products of his Jewishness, but readers are not obliged to share his view. Indeed, they are invited to understand that the suffering and the comedy of Alexander Portnoy are the suffering and the comedy of modern man, who seeks and finds explanations for his plight but is unable to resolve it, whose understanding is as limited as his sense of possibility."[11] The essential difference between Portnoy's and Roth's opinions on Jewishness is a matter of focus and emphasis. The neurotic Portnoy, in typically egotistical and self-obsessed fashion, adopts a purely personal response, emitting a protracted diatribe that amounts to a renunciation of his ethnicity. But Roth's purpose in writing the novel was more broad-ranging and certainly more constructive than that. In creating a protagonist who has had the misfortune to have been psychologically damaged by his particular experience of Jewish life, Roth presents a case that is extreme—indeed, the book is finally about extremity—but which is believable. And in so doing, Roth is not himself renouncing the Jewish experience, but criticizing what he believes it to have become in some cases. Portnoy, himself an exaggeration, rejects; Roth exaggerates to dissect.

Elsewhere, Roth's treatment of his characters' Jewishness is quite different. Often there is even a strong sense of ethnic pride, an almost celebratory quality that seems to validate his claim, "I have always been far more pleased by my good fortune in being born a Jew than my critics may begin to imagine."[12] Works such as "'I Always Wanted You to Admire My Fasting': or Looking at Kafka," the "Salad Days" section of *My Life as a Man, The Breast, The Professor of Desire,* and others are obviously imbued with retrospective affection for the wholeheartedness of Jewish homelife, while earlier stories such as "Defender of the Faith" and "Eli, the Fanatic," despite the labels of anti-Semitism that have sometimes been applied to them, are clear-cut endorsements of the Jewish tradition.

If in certain works Roth's depiction of the Jewish-American experience is censorious, it most certainly is not always so. And as he himself has pointed out, the criticisms that he does formulate "may even be a way to redeem the facts, to give them the weight and value that they should have in the world, rather than the disproportionate significance they obviously have for some misguided . . . people."[13] Ultimately, however, Roth is less concerned with such considerations than with achieving fidelity to his own (somewhat turbulent) experience, and the disciplined rendering of his vision in credible fictions. If the criticisms directed at Roth are partially justified, he is nevertheless correct in discounting those objections to his work, for it is the prerogative—indeed, the obligation—of artists to respond to life strictly on their own terms. As Henry James said, we must be willing to grant an author's donnée, and evaluate only in terms of what is made of it. As a Jewish-American writer, Roth uses ethnicity as a framework or context within which to portray contemporary reality, and in his best works has done so with great skill.

Just as Roth employs a Jewish reference frame, Updike, too, operates within a specific and highly personal cultural context. But as a chronicler of the Protestant middle class,

Updike has attracted little of the controversy that surrounds
Roth, because he is exempt from the often problematic demands of group solidarity that burden a minority writer. A
member of the "ruling class" majority, Updike is at liberty to
assail the status quo without incurring hostility; indeed, in a
nontotalitarian society, the serious writer who addresses the
community at large is almost expected to assume the role of
judgmental commentator.

Updike's work partakes of a long tradition of American
Protestant self-criticism, and is in this sense akin to that of
Hawthorne, Howells, Twain, Lewis, Steinbeck, and others.
Like his predecessors, however, Updike does not attack
American Christianity itself, but the distortion or violation of
its tenets. Just as Roth berates his characters for failing to
maintain the dignity of their Jewish heritage, Updike assails
the abrogation of Christian values. The difference, of course,
is that Roth's intentions have been in part misconstrued because of the quite understandable vigilance and the protec-
tive self-monitoring exercised by the much-abused ethnic
group of which he is a part, while Updike's message has been
characteristically "tolerated"—and thereby, in effect, ig-
nored—by the smugly complacent cultural mainstream to
which he belongs.

Much like Roth, Updike perceives in contemporary
America a widespread loss of spiritual substance, a diminu-
tion that finds its outward manifestations in cultural vulgarity and an empty, materialistic value system. He repeatedly
suggests that the breakdown of religious belief has occasioned
a generalized malaise, and that our tacit acceptance of the
"death of God" has caused many of our current problems.
There has been a tendency in the twentieth century to gradu-
ally replace traditional religion with secular surrogates, and
Updike's novels and stories consistently portray confused,

questing, unfulfilled characters bereft of the spiritual fortifi-
cation that sustained earlier generations. This partly explains
Updike's professed and obvious penchant for juxtaposing
images of the present with evocations of the American past.
He has frequently drawn upon the experiences of his early
childhood and adolescence, focusing on the fictional Olinger,
Pennsylvania (significantly pronounced "O-Linger," and
based on Updike's hometown of Shillington). Updike's fond
handling of the Olinger material is akin to Roth's similarly
warm treatment of childhood experiences, be they actual (as
in *Portnoy's Complaint* and the essay "Beyond the Last Rope")
or invented (as in *The Professor of Desire*). In Updike's depictions of the present, there is little of the warmth or poignancy
that permeates the Olinger-based works. Whenever Updike
departs from the Olinger context to portray sophisticated,
upwardly mobile city dwellers and suburbanites, and in the
"Rabbit" novels, where his subject is the blue collar proletar-
iat of urban Brewer (Reading), Pennsylvania, his censure of
present-day America is plainly evident.

In the representative early short story "Toward Evening,"
for example, there is a highly symbolic scene in which Rafe,
the protagonist, whimsically associates skyscraper numbers
on Broadway with calendar years. The implied comment on
contemporary society (and its future prospects) is quite direct: "The clearly marked numbers on the east side of the
street ran: 1832, 1836, 1846, 1850 (Wordsworth dies), 1880
(great Nihilist trial in Saint Petersburg), 1900 (Rafe's father
born in Trenton), 1902 (Braque leaves Le Havre to study
painting in Paris), 1914 (Joyce begins *Ulysses;* war begins in
Europe), 1926 (Rafe's parents marry in Ithaca), 1936 (Rafe
is four years old). Where the present should have stood, a
block was torn down, and the numbering began again with
2000, a boring progressive edifice."[14] Similarly, in the im-

pressionistic autobiographical memoir "The Blessed Man of Boston, My Grandmother's Thimble, and Fanning Island," Updike says of his grandmother that "the land which cast her up was harsher, more sparsely exploited, more fertile than it is now. That she was unique; that she came toward the end of the time when uniqueness was possible. Already identical faces throng the street."[15] With characteristic acumen, the British critic Tony Tanner has observed that in Updike's work there is a sense of "continuous erosion," a pervasive apprehension of waste and disintegration that provides an unlikely link with writers such as John Barth and William Burroughs.[16] This preoccupation with loss and social decay finds repeated expression throughout Updike's oeuvre—frequently given metaphorical embodiment in the odd and unpleasant image of dental decay—but most persuasively in *Couples* and the "Rabbit" novels, where cultural disintegration is most clearly associated with the breakdown of Christian religion.

In *Couples,* a lengthy treatment of ten adulterous suburban Massachusetts marriages, the inhabitants of this "post-pill paradise"[17] make a religion of sex. Certainly the implication is that such a development is not to be desired: the book is clearly an indictment of upper middle class suburbia, as are Updike's several complementary Tarbox short stories. In *Couples* the characters cling to an anachronistic sense of W.A.S.P. class privilege but have abandoned all vestiges of Christian morality. The non-Protestants (the Gallaghers, the Constantines, the Saltzes, and the Ongs) are separated from the others by "a delicate social line" (p. 226). Protagonist Piet Hanema—a laboring man—is accepted only because his wife "had been a Hamilton" (p. 12). But despite the principal couples' social pretensions, they have totally lost sight of the Protestant ethic that sustained their forebears. Like the secularized Jews of Woodenton (another symbolically named suburbia) in Roth's "Eli, the Fanatic," these people have fallen prey to a materialistic despiritualization that has robbed their lives of meaning. Piet's assessment of contemporary society is correct when he asserts, "I think America now is like an unloved child smothered in candy. . . . God doesn't love us any more. . . . We're fat and full of pimples and always whining for more candy. We've fallen from grace" (p. 200). Updike lends this judgment added symbolic weight, relating it to the couples' new "religion" of empty sensuality when Piet later observes a "condom and candy wrapper. . . paired in the . . . gutter" (p. 378).

Although *Couples* is weakened by a certain superficiality of characterization, it nevertheless is an emphatic illustration of Updike's concern with the rejection of religion in our time. The book also suggests, as do so many of Updike's works, that perhaps institutionalized religion has contributed to its own demise by responding inadequately to the needs of the modern age. At the book's conclusion we learn that when the rubble of the burned Congregationalist church is examined, the "old church proved not only badly gutted but structurally unsound: a miracle it had not collapsed of itself a decade ago" (p. 457).

In the "Rabbit" novels, too, Updike implies that institutionalized religion has degenerated into a self-parodying ineffectuality. Although Harry "Rabbit" Angstrom of *Rabbit, Run* is a confused, self-centered, and frequently insensitive individual whose sense of interpersonal obligation and moral responsibility is at best only partially developed, he possesses an intuitive awareness of spiritual mystery, an antinomian incandescence that sets him sharply apart from the drab world of grimily industrial Brewer and its pinched, unimaginative populace. He is sincere in attributing his need to "run"—i.e., to seek personal freedom—to a basically religious yearning. Like Piet Hanema, but far-more convincingly, he is portrayed as a knight-errant in quest of a metaphysical grail.

But he runs in a void. Those around him all misunderstand, or fail to perceive, his sense of wonder and his vaguely comprehended but strongly felt intimations of Something Beyond. "Well I don't know all this about theology," he says to the young minister, Eccles, "but I'll tell you. I *do* feel . . . that somewhere . . . there's something that wants me to find it."[18] Eccles, although genuinely sympathetic, cannot relate to Rabbit's visionary impulses, because in actuality he does not share Rabbit's intensity of conviction. Indeed, he finally confesses, "I don't believe in anything" (p. 267). Conversely, the Reverend Mr. Kruppenbach, the book's other clergyman, espouses the same sort of unquestioning faith that Rabbit unknowingly embodies, but also fails to appreciate Rabbit's spiritual component. He dismisses Rabbit as "a *Schussel*" (p. 169), or foolish wastrel. In their failure to assist Rabbit, the two ministers personify the contemporary church's generalized failure. By emphasizing the unproductive parrying that occurs between Rabbit and Eccles (i.e., "ecclesiastic"), Updike focuses his critical lens most directly on the increasingly futile attempts of religious institutions to provide a stable reference point for the American middle class. In one highly symbolic scene, Rabbit looks toward the once bright stained-glass church window that has previously afforded him a measure of spiritual solace. Now, however, it is dim, "a dark circle in a stone façade" (p. 306).

Updike's vision of collective spiritual emptiness is developed at still greater length in the novel's highly topical sequel, *Rabbit Redux,* published eleven years later, just after the social upheaval of the 1960s. Once again, but in far greater

detail than ever before, Updike depicts a kitsch-strewn vista
bare of moral guideposts. Harry Angstrom, now thirty-six,
has become a pale reflection of his former self, having settled
into a bland and spiritless conservatism that has transformed
him into a cliché-mouthing drone. The Harry of 1969 (the
book covers the summer and fall of that year) has settled for a
humdrum existence that revolves around his job as a typesetter, his flimsy ranch house in a Brewer suburb, and his simplistic endorsement of a platitudinous pseudopatriotism. Although on the most obvious level the book's title is simply an
indication that it is a sequel to *Rabbit, Run,* the Latin adjec-
tive "redux" also connotes "restoration," and in medical usage indicates recuperation. The novel is aptly titled, then,
because to a large extent it chronicles Harry's revivification.
Through a (somewhat unlikely) embroilment with a Lolita-
like teenaged runaway and a volatile black militant, Harry
experiences spiritual rebirth, mends his recently broken marriage, and achieves a level of self-knowledge.

Certainly one of the most involved and ambitious of Updike's novels, *Rabbit Redux* is at once a relevant social document and an interesting artistic achievement. Updike uses
specific historical facts—the moon shots, the sexual revolu-
tion, the drug explosion, black militancy, and the emergence
of women's self-determination—both to comment on the
state of the nation and to provide a context for Harry's regeneration. Foremost among Updike's themes, however, is the
idea that as conventional religion has been abandoned, we
have fallen prey to various embodiments of the Antichrist, a
god of chaos, destruction, and despair. Just as in *Rabbit, Run*
Harry had to contend with the tepid, ineffectual Christianity
of the Reverend Mr. Eccles, he has in *Rabbit Redux* to respond
somehow to the fanatical Skeeter Farnsworth, who an-
nounces himself as "*the* Black Jesus."[19] Of God, Skeeter says

that "Chaos is His holy face" (p. 261), and he preaches a secular gospel based on hate and negation. Harry correctly assesses Skeeter as "religious-crazy" (p. 328). But Harry par-
ticipates, along with his young son Nelson and the runaway
Jill, in Skeeter's nightly "seminars" on such topics as race,
religion, and morality, while they partake of marijuana, the
"sacrament" of the "Church of Skeeter."

Religious allusions abound, as Skeeter becomes an almost
Yeatsian embodiment of the apocalyptic "second coming."
And therein lies the central paradox of the novel's treatment
of Christianity. Updike seems to imply that America has so
lost sight of traditional Christian virtue that only through the
agency of evil can Harry hope to recapture his lost spirituality. Moreover, there is a degree of validity in much of what
Skeeter says, his virulence notwithstanding. Updike indicates that America has created many of its own problems by
permitting social injustice and inequality, in violation of the
tenets of Christian brotherhood. While Harry's childhood
conception of "the American Dream"—"God lying sleeping, the quilt-colored map of the U.S. coming out of his head
like a cloud" (p. 114)—is obviously a fantasy, Skeeter's is
more accurate, in view of the nation's treatment of racial mi-
norities: "this place was never such a place it was a *dream,* it
was a state of mind from those poor fool pilgrims on, right?"
(p. 242). By the conclusion of *Rabbit Redux,* through Skeeter's
dark agency, Harry has glimpsed truth. Harry seems to have
been "led back" to a clearer self-concept and an increased
understanding of life, but only by having wrestled with evil.
Harry's house is burned (just as the church in *Couples* is), and
the suggestion is that only through extreme rites of purification will righteousness prevail now that we have lost sight of
the more accustomed paths to salvation.

Rabbit Is Rich, the third installment of the Rabbit saga, is a
far less intense and volatile book than either *Rabbit, Run* or *Rabbit Redux.* Yet its criticisms are no less pointed. Indeed, the
rather understated aura of weary resignation that permeates
this novel helps to convey its message, for the facetiously-
titled *Rabbit Is Rich* is ultimately about poverty—a spiritual
poverty that is both Harry's and America's. Plaintive ironies
abound as Harry—although ten years older than in *Rabbit
Redux* and now financially solvent—is really far poorer, meta-
physically, than in the past. He has inherited his father-in-
law's automobile dealership and commands an adequate in-
come. He has joined a country club and golfs regularly; as
the novel unfolds he vacations in the islands, invests in gold
and silver, and moves to the suburbs. But his new prosperity
leaves him less fulfilled than he has ever been, for he has in effect "sold out," and has thereby lost almost all the spontaneity and verve that once set him apart.

In *Rabbit, Run,* old Mrs. Smith tells Harry, "That's what
you have, Harry: life" (p. 223); but *Rabbit Is Rich* is obsessed
with death. Although death is very much present in both *Rabbit, Run* and *Rabbit Redux,* in *Rabbit Is Rich* it becomes a dominant, central motif, along with economic inflation. Simply
stated, the novel limns a world in which, paradoxically,
"more is less"; both Harry and America at large have embraced delusions of progress and success, but really both are,
in the book's opening words, "running out of gas."[20]

Even Harry's once-keen sexual appetite has abated, as a
generalized complacency has blunted virtually every aspect
of his life. Appropriately, his venture into spouse-swapping
with two of the other country club couples ends in frustration. The woman he craves chooses a different lover (whom
Harry despises), and Harry is left with that man's wife

(whom Harry finds unattractive); meanwhile, Harry's wife Janice joins with a man who proves to be sexually superior to Harry. That this episode occurs at all is yet another index of Harry's essential shortsightedness, for really his only true prosperity is in his marriage to Janice, who has grown as Harry has dwindled. And Harry himself knows that "she is his fortune" (p. 384), "the keystone of his wealth. . . . [she is] his stubborn prize" (p. 455).

Harry's erratic behavior derives not only from his own confusions but also from the societal muddle that surrounds him. The book becomes at once a domestic comedy and a sociological record as Updike details the hideous cultural vulgarity in which Harry is mired and to which he has now almost completely acquiesced. As his son Nelson laments, "Dad doesn't like to look bad anymore, that was one thing about him in the old days you could admire, that he didn't care that much how he looked from the outside, what the neighbors thought . . . he had this crazy dim faith in himself. . . . That spark is gone, leaving a big dead man" (p. 314). Nelson's feelings are strikingly similar to Harry's upon learning of Skeeter's death in a shoot-out with police: "a certain light was withdrawn from the world, a daring, a promise that all would be overturned. . . . That part of him subject to Skeeter's spell had shriveled and been overlaid" (pp. 31–32). The suggestion is that Harry has been simply worn down by contending with contemporary life in all of its exhausting vacuity. And of course, Updike once again assails institutionalized religion for its failure to serve as a bulwark.

The Reverend Mr. Archie Campbell, the novel's one clergyman, is an obvious homosexual whose ministry is characterized by a glib, cavalier expediency. And Harry, although he dislikes Campbell, is an accomplice to the minister's imposture; he watches admiringly at Nelson's "shotgun" wedding, marveling at Campbell "gathering and pressing the straggle of guests into a congregation, subduing any fear that this ceremony might be a farce" (p. 243). Updike's distaste is everywhere apparent, and at one point the church is described as "a kind of wreck wherein many Americans have died" (p. 240). In works like *Couples* and the "Rabbit" novels, Updike portrays a state of affairs that he had predicted in his first novel, *The Poorhouse Fair.* I have argued elsewhere that in retrospect that book can be seen as a sort of thesis statement for Updike's whole subsequent corpus.[21] *The Poorhouse Fair* stresses the importance of orthodox Christian faith as a stay against confusion, while predicting "the collapse of public morale and the spiritual reduction of the whole country to a 'poorhouse.'"[22] Surely *Rabbit Is Rich*—the irony of the title is again germane—describes such a spiritually impoverished culture, a moral wilderness bereft of meaning and purpose.

Roth has said that although he makes no pretense of speaking for American Jews, he certainly speaks *to* them, and Updike has similarly identified his intended audience.[23] "When I write," he told the *Paris Review*, "I aim in my mind not toward New York but toward a vague spot a little to the east of Kansas."[24] As Roth addresses the Jewish-American community, often castigating what he considers its failures and excesses, Updike is no less the critical gadfly, isolating and dissecting those features of mainstream W.A.S.P. culture that he deems deficient. He "speaks to the nation which he knows as his—his to love, his to grieve over . . . it is the failure of Protestantism that he traces."[25] In the work of each writer, there is a very perceptible blend of both affection for and dissatisfaction with the particular American ethos that his works embody, reflect, and comment upon. Both Roth and Updike are deeply concerned with matters of religious and ethnic identity, an area of interest that strongly colors—and largely determines—their respective artistic perspectives.

3

Fathers and Sons: Family Relationships in Roth and Updike

A MAJOR THEME treated by both Roth and Updike is the difficulty of close interpersonal dealings, especially between parents and children. Of course, this subject has been of perennial concern to novelists, but in the work of these two authors it is absolutely central. Both writers view family relationships as extremely problematic and essentially frustrating but acknowledge their importance in human affairs and return to them repeatedly as a subject for fiction.

Perhaps the most significant assumption shared by Roth and Updike is that in all relationships the individual ultimately stands alone. In their fiction, the traditional ideas of family solidarity and reinforcement of personal identity through strong familial bonds appear to have lost their viability. Nowhere is this more bleakly apparent than in their most recent books. For example, the protagonist of Roth's *Zuckerman Unbound* exists in a familial void; childless and twice divorced, he has been spurned by his brother and cursed by his dying father. In *The Anatomy Lesson,* he has been divorced a third time, is depressed about his estrangement from his brother, and is mourning his recently deceased mother. The parents of Updike's Harry Angstrom in *Rabbit Is Rich* are already dead, his marriage lacks true commitment, and his relationship with his son is poisoned by virulent mutual hostility. Roth and Updike seem to be suggesting that in the fragmented modern world we are left almost entirely to our own devices, cut off from even the most basic sources of communion. However, neither writer celebrates this idea. On the contrary, much of their work constitutes a lament for these lost wellsprings of security, solace, and strength. Their protagonists' confusions are rendered all the more vexing by the loss of vital personal ties and the concomitant sense of guilt and unworthiness that such a rupture engenders.

In Roth's novels, this predicament is dramatically obvious. While Portnoy, for example, blames his problems on his Jewishness, in so doing he denies his parents and in fact openly castigates them—the mother, especially—throughout his rambling diatribe. This renunciation is not without its price. As a consequence, Portnoy experiences extreme self-hatred, fueled largely by mixed feelings of love and hatred toward his parents—feelings that he can neither exorcise nor accept. Similarly, Neil Klugman of *Goodbye, Columbus,* in rejecting the old-world Jewishness of Newark, also rejects his surrogate parents, Aunt Gladys and Uncle Max. Like Portnoy, Neil feels the wrench. Both characters frequently reveal deep affection for their families, even while criticizing them. Portnoy's poignant cry "This is my mother and father I'm talking about" (p. 30) has much in common with Neil's wistful references to his aunt and uncle, "sharing a Mounds bar in the cindery darkness of their alley, on beach chairs."[1]

This theme runs throughout Roth's canon, receiving its most somber treatment in the "Zuckerman" novels. In *The Ghost Writer,* young Nathan Zuckerman has written a short story that has incurred his father's wrath, and the fledgling author seeks a surrogate father in the person of E. I. Lonoff, an established writer. Yet Zuckerman's fantasized marriage to Anne Frank reveals the intensity of his subconscious desire for family sanction. As mentioned above, in *Zuckerman Unbound* the protagonist—now a well-known writer himself—is cursed by his father from the latter's deathbed, leaving Zuckerman "no longer any man's son" (p. 224), thereby ending the novel on a profoundly negative note. And these fundamental disruptions continue to haunt Zuckerman in *The Anatomy Lesson.* Conversely, Roth's most uplifting treatment of the father-son theme occurs in *The Professor of Desire.* David Kepesh and his father enjoy a warm, mutually tolerant friendship which, although not without its conflicts, ultimately constitutes a source of fulfillment for both men. But the Kepeshes are the exception; in virtually every other instance in Roth's fiction, father and son are at loggerheads.

Small wonder, then, that Roth chose lines from Wallace Steven's "Æsthétique du Mal" for one of the epigraphs to his first full-length novel, *Letting Go;* the selection reads in part, "The Son / And the father alike and equally are spent, / Each one, by the necessity of being / Himself." The emphasis in this very Jamesian novel is upon individual consciousness and the moral and psychological ramifications of complicated interpersonal responses. *Letting Go* chronicles several years in the lives of five confused and unhappy people: Gabe Wallach, a young academic whose successful graduate career leads to a university professorship; Wallach's father, a prosperous dentist and recent widower; Paul Herz, a harrassed colleague of Gabe's; Libby, Herz's sickly, neurotic wife; and Martha Regenhart, a struggling divorcee with whom Gabe has an affair. But such capsule descriptions of the principals fail to convey the complexity of their many entanglements, both with each other and with a host of minor characters. The various dilemmas of Gabe Wallach and company are but imperfectly resolved, for the causes of these people's problems are rooted in universal human conflicts: tensions between lovers, between husbands and wives, and, of course, between parents and children.

All of sometime narrator Gabe Wallach's dealings are attempts to fathom the ambivalences of mutual responsibility, to discover an answer to the elemental questions posed by Hillel: "If I am not for myself, who will be? If I am only for myself, what am I?"[2] This basic tension surfaces early in the novel in Gabe's impossible relationship with his father. The disconsolate elder Wallach is typical of practically all the fathers in Roth's work. Like the fathers of Portnoy, Tarnopol, and Zuckerman, Dr. Wallach does not fully understand his son, and suffers greatly from the sense of strained artificiality that thwarts their attempts at communication. Nevertheless, like most of Roth's other Jewish fathers, he is an endearing character. Self-sacrificing and right-thinking, Dr. Wallach is a strong, virile, decent man who is not without sensitivity and wisdom. His too-protective meddling in Gabe's affairs is the result only of his love for his son. Yet Gabe greatly resents what he interprets as his father's attempts to control his life.

Sons in Roth's books are typically impatient with their irrepressible fathers. Even David Kepesh's father (like Dr. Wallach, a recent widower) becomes an embodiment of tragicomic parental intensity, finally prompting Kepesh to remark wonderingly to himself, "Until death do us part—the tremendous closeness and the tremendous distance between my father and myself will . . . continue in the same perplexing proportions as have existed all our lives."[3] Roth's portrayals not only of actual fathers, but also of older men generally (i.e., "father figures") tend to be uniformly approving, even if his young protagonists do not always see their elders that way. Often, for example, a character's uncle or older brother acts as a surrogate father—Paul Herz's Uncle Jerry in *Letting Go,* Tarnopol's brother Moe in *My Life as a Man*— and is presented in a favorable light, offering advice and guidance to his confused junior. Almost always, the "older man" in Roth's fiction, as in Hemingway's, is a wisdom figure—almost a Bellovian "reality instructor." Certainly Ben Patimkin, the father of Neil Klugman's lover Brenda, functions this way in *Goodbye, Columbus*.

Although Neil Klugman is somewhat intimidated by Patimkin, he remarks that "Mr. Patimkin reminded me of my father, except that when he spoke he did not surround each syllable with a wheeze. He was tall, strong, ungrammatical, and a ferocious eater. When he attacked his salad . . . the veins swelled under the heavy skin of his forearm" (p. 31); this is certainly an admiring description. Further, Patimkin is clearly on excellent, loving terms with all of his children, and is in fact more reminiscent of Newark than of Short Hills: "Mr. Patimkin sat on the grass at the far end of the court. He took his shirt off, and in his undershirt, and his whole day's growth of beard, looked like a trucker. Brenda's old nose fitted him well. There was a bump in it, all right; up at the bridge it seemed as though a small eight-sided diamond had been squeezed in under the skin. I knew Mr. Patimkin would never bother to have that stone cut from his face, and yet, with joy and pride, no doubt, had paid to have Brenda's diamond removed" (p. 38).

At another point Neil remarks that "Mr. Patimkin is not wholly successful in stifling a belch, though the failure even more than the effort ingratiates him to me" (p. 34). Having achieved hard-won success through his own strenuous efforts, Ben Patimkin is not corrupted by it and refuses to adopt the social "airs" of the *nouveaux riches*. Despite Neil's tendency to adopt a condescending tone toward virtually everyone else, he obviously respects Patimkin and regrets that there is no common ground on which they can meet. Visiting the sink company that Patimkin owns and runs, Neil recriminates: "Suppose Mr. Patimkin should come up to me and say, 'Okay, boy, you want to marry my daughter, let's see what you can do.' Well, he would see: in a moment that floor would be a shattered mosaic, a crunchy path of enamel. 'Klugman, what kind of worker are you? You work like you eat!' 'That's right, that's right, I'm a sparrow, let me go'" (p. 103).

Watching Patimkin transact business on the telephone, Neil recognizes the man's drive and expertise. And Neil discerns that Patimkin's brusqueness is simply a mask, that beneath his gruff exterior there is real feeling, particularly toward his family. Neil's grudging affection for the older man is unmistakable: "these few words he did speak could hardly transmit all the satisfaction and surprise he felt about the life he had managed to build for himself and his family. . . . 'When I got married we had forks and knives from the five and ten. This kid [his son Ron] needs gold to eat off,' but there was no anger; far from it" (pp. 105–6).

Patimkin is a convenient example of Roth's tendency to provide an older character who serves as a sort of moral arbiter, but others abound. Another such character, although he actually *says* very little, is Mr. Barbatnik, the concentration camp survivor in *The Professor of Desire*. The "Zuckerman" novels also employ this device, as E. I. Lonoff in *The Ghost Writer*, the literary agent Andre Schevitz in *Zuckerman Unbound*, and the "dolorologist," Dr. Kotler, in *The Anatomy Lesson* all provide fatherly assurance and encouragement to the floundering Zuckerman. And of course, Roth's fictional analysts, Spielvogel and Klinger, serve in precisely this way, as befitting their professional role.

Roth's depiction of Dr. Wallach in *Letting Go* is consistent, then, with his tendency to portray father figures warmly. Like Jack Portnoy and Abe Kepesh, Dr. Wallach well-meaningly beleaguers his son, harrassing Gabe with long-distance telephone calls to Iowa, where Gabe is a graduate student in literature:

Two or three evenings a week my father and I had the same phone conversation, pointless on the surface, pleading beneath. The old man stood being familyless all day, what with having his patients' mouths to look into; it was alone with his avocado and lettuce dinner that he broke down. When he called his voice shook; when he hung up—or when I did—his vibrato passed directly into the few meager objects in the room. . . . The trouble with the phone calls, in fact, was that all the time I felt it necessary to the preservation of my life and sanity to resist the old man, I understood how it was for him sitting in that huge Victorian living room all alone.[4]

Gabe's relationship with his father continues in this way even after Gabe accepts a position at the University of Chicago. And although Gabe confesses at one point, "I had been missing my father as much as he had been missing me" (p. 28), the necessity of living one's own life, of "letting go" of family ties, presents irreconcilable problems.

As a consequence, even their time spent together during Gabe's holiday visits to New York is characterized by mutual discomfort. An atmosphere of strained artificiality is sharply evoked in Gabe's description of a tennis match at the West Side Athletic Club: "We two Wallach men, my father and I, stood in place on the tennis court, pushing dull lifeless shots back and forth at one another. Each of us had been trying for over an hour not to inconvenience his opponent by so much

as a foot. For four days now, life—off the court as well as on—
had consisted of just this sort of polite emotionless volleying"
(p. 33). Of course, the discomfort of the relationship is
caused by love, and this is what makes the situation so difficult. Both men are stymied by the intricacies of the paternal
and filial bonds. At one point, after Gabe grants his father's
request to examine his teeth, he experiences a not uncharacteristic surge of affection for his father: "Then his face ap-
peared above my own. I could have pulled him down and
kissed him. But would he understand that I was not prepared
to surrender my life to his? He was a wholehearted man, and
such people are hard to kiss half-heartedly" (p. 39).

Likewise, Dr. Wallach is aware of Gabe's needs:

All sons. All sons leave their fathers. Of course. He considered himself a student of psychology and he was not naïve about certain facts
of life. Just the other day on the beach he had had an interesting discussion about parental problems with Abe Cole. . . . He had told
Abe . . . that unhappy as he had been when his son had gone off
for good, he had known in his heart that a boy does not become a
man living in his father's house. . . . he believed that he said—
children grow up and go away. That was one of life's laws to which
he and his son could not expect to be made exceptions. Nevertheless . . . there *are* certain circumstances, are there not? Special predicaments people wind up in that are not of their own choosing and
that both child and parent have to recognize and make accommo-
dations for? If only his son . . . had had an *ounce* of patience with
him; if only he himself had displayed an ounce of control (p. 487).

Yet there can be no total reconciliation. The father is finally
able to relinquish his grip on Gabe only after he himself has
remarried. Ironically, Gabe then resents his stepmother, at
least partly because he is jealous of the attention that his father lavishes upon her. *Letting Go* seems to suggest that conflict is inevitable in close interpersonal relationships and that

human dealings are intrinsically and unavoidably enigmatic, especially within the family circle.

But as Judith Paterson Jones and Guinevera A. Nance have observed in an excellent recent study, Roth's "most pessimistic portrayal of the family" appears in one of his least read and most underrated books, his "Gentile experiment," *When She Was Good.*[5] The book's midwestern ambiance and its female protagonist make it a most unrepresentative production, yet *When She Was Good* is in many ways a probing exploration of family tensions. Comparing this work to *Portnoy's Complaint,* Roth has said that "an alert reader familiar with both books might find in them a similar preoccupation with the warfare between parents and children." Likening protagonist Lucy Nelson to Portnoy, Roth has termed her "in her imprisoning passion and in the role she assumes of the enraged offspring, very much his soul mate."[6]

Lucy shares with Portnoy, and with Roth's other male protagonists, a tendency to assess life by illusory criteria; like so many of Updike's W.A.S.P.'s, Roth's Lucy finds that the actual circumstances of her existence fall far short of the naïvely optimistic versions of American life that she has absorbed. Specifically, Lucy disapproves of her family. Although they are in fact a rather lacklustre contingent—her father is a drinker, her mother is weakly self-abnegating, and her young husband is somewhat immature and directionless—they are by no means contemptible. Yet Lucy, having totally subscribed to the popular, mythical ideal of the "perfect" family, will settle for nothing less, and her outraged self-righteousness toward her family's shortcomings is as self-defeating as it is strident.

Like everyone else in symbolically (and ironically) named Liberty Center, Lucy has been subliminally conditioned from birth to imagine as normal the sort of domestic bliss pictured by Norman Rockwell on the covers of the old *Saturday Evening Post*. Unlike most other people, however, Lucy really believes in this form of the American Dream, and fails to recognize it for the idealized inflation that it actually is. Like Portnoy, Wallach, et al., Lucy not only takes herself quite seriously, but places unrealistically stringent demands on those around her as well. When her family fail to measure up, she rages. In her dealings with the men in her life—her grandfather, her father, her uncle, her husband—she is particularly exacting: "she idealises the masculine role to the extent of ruining it. Wanting men to be 'protectors and defenders, heroes and saviours', she finds them 'philanderers and frauds, cowards and weaklings, cheaters and liars'—without realizing that her own violent demands on authority have made authority impossible. Even her grandfather must repeat 'I am not God', while he tries and fails to convince her that he cannot totally control other people or their problems."[7] And this, of course, is directly related to the novel's indictment of the destructive consequences of our culture's "furious insistence on the family as a unit," our communal belief that "the system must continue" at all costs.[8]

As Jones and Nance point out, Lucy is "the tragic victim of a social milieu . . . based on the patriarchal concept of the male as protector . . . in a family in which the males who purport to protect are powerless to do so."[9] The parallels to *Portnoy's Complaint* are obvious, as revealed by this passage from the opening section of that novel:

We are on the big dirt field back of my school. He sets his collection book on the ground, and steps up to the plate in his coat and his brown fedora. He wears square steel-rimmed spectacles, and his hair (which now I wear) is a wild bush the color and texture of steel wool; and those teeth, which sit all night long in a glass in the bathroom smiling at the toilet bowl, now smile out at me, his beloved, his flesh and his blood, the little boy upon whose head no rain shall ever fall. "Okay, Big Shot Ballplayer," he says, and grasps my new regulation bat somewhere near the middle—and to my astonishment, with his left hand where his right hand should be. I am suddenly overcome with such sadness: I want to tell him, *Hey, your hands are wrong,* but am unable to, for fear I might begin to cry—or he might! "Come on, Big Shot, throw the ball," he calls, and so I do—and of course discover that on top of all the other things I am just beginning to suspect about my father, he isn't "King Kong" Charlie Keller either.

Some umbrella. (pp. 10–11)

Roth seems to imply that many of modern America's ills stem from a collective tendency to exalt the family out of all proportion to its actual powers as a social institution. Too much family, too much "love," Roth suggests, is as destructive as too little. This idea appears in *Portnoy's Complaint* and elsewhere in Roth's fiction, but it is the major thesis of *When She Was Good.* Here it takes on an additional dimension, too, for Lucy's simplistic, overly literal habits of mind apply not just to her family dealings, but generally to her whole outlook on life. Roth did not intend Lucy as a totally representative case, he says, but he believes that hers is a not-uncommon personality: "it has always seemed to me that though we are, to be sure, not a nation of Lucy Nelsons, there is a strong American inclination to respond to life *like* a Lucy Nelson— an inclination to reduce the complexities and mysteries of living to the most simple-minded and childish issues of right and wrong. . . . What destroys Lucy (some readers may hold) has nothing whatsoever to do with the rest of us. I am of a different opinion."[10] In this sense, especially, Roth's treatment of family problems in *When She Was Good* is somewhat unusual, rising beyond the personal level to the broadly cultural application, as in Updike's handlings of the same themes.

In Updike's work the elemental tensions surrounding interactions between parents and children are just as fundamental as they are in Roth's. Tony Tanner identifies as Updike's principal themes "marriage, children, the relationship
between generations, and the difficulties . . . of familial con-
tinuity."[11] This is quite correct, as practically all of Updike's
protagonists, like Roth's, are locked into extremely complex,
psychologically demanding family relationships that in many
cases become Updike's principal subject. Updike himself has
said that "domestic fierceness within the middle class"[12] is
among his main topics. In Updike's Olinger stories, for example, as well as in *The Centaur* and *Of the Farm,* the parent-
child interplay is a central concern, just as marriage provides
the subject of *Couples, Marry Me,* and the short story collections *Too Far to Go* and *Problems.*

Updike seems to suggest that the problems his characters
experience reflect a larger cultural phenomenon—the disintegration of W.A.S.P. America. In Updike's fictional world,
family relationships are rendered all the more difficult by the
fact that the persons involved exist in a period of shifting values and changing assumptions. The fictional Olinger itself
becomes a metaphor for the lost past, a time when (at least in
the narrators' imaginations) life was simpler, more easily de-
cipherable, and governed by received systems of response.
He has remarked that "as a child, I lived what was to become
my material and message,"[13] and it is in the works that center
on Olinger and Rabbit's Brewer that Updike most effectively
explores his family-centered themes.

In each of the Olinger stories, in *The Centaur,* and in *Of the
Farm,* a sensitive young protagonist is torn between the slowly dwindling, small-town world of his parents and the attractions of the larger realm of possibility that lies beyond and
which his aspirations lead him toward. Whether he is a teen-

aged boy like Allen Dow of "Flight" or Peter Caldwell of *The Centaur,* or a young adult like Joey Robinson of *Of the Farm,* his dealings with his parents are characterized by mixed emotions and a concomitant sense of strain. Although in every case the protagonist's parents entertain high hopes for his future, and although the son shares these visions of grandeur, there are almost always guilt feelings experienced by the son for wishing to transcend his parents' station, and at times there is a sort of unwilled jealousy or resentment evinced by the mother toward the son.

The opening pages of "Flight" are representative: as they survey the town of Olinger from a nearby hilltop, Allen Dow's mother tells him, "There we all are, and there we'll all be forever. . . . Except you, Allen. You're going to fly." But on another occasion the mother admonishes him, "You'll never learn, you'll stick and die in the dirt just like I'm doing. Why should you be better than your mother?"[14] These families live at an extremely high emotional pitch. The protagonist's mother is always a formidable figure, melodramatic and strong-willed, at once supportive and emasculating, while the father is typically a long-suffering, self-deprecating altruist whose quirky behavior is as much a product of willed, defensive idiosyncrasy as of genuine eccentricity. The Olinger parents seem to have embraced self-parody as a stay against the vicissitudes of existence. Realizing that their small-town context is fast becoming obsolete in an age of technology and mass society, they take refuse in extremes of theatricality that are designed both to mask their insecurities and to provide an arena in which to grope toward workable philosophies of life. Allen Dow describes himself as a "child who had been surrounded all his life by adults ransacking each other for the truth" (pp. 68–69), and this significant line is applicable to the other Olinger protagonists as well.

Interestingly, however, this tumultuous homelife is invariably presented as stimulating, nourishing, and fortifying, and is described in terms of fondly wistful recollection. One Olinger protagonist says, for example, that he "always awoke to the sound of my parents talking, voices which even in agreement were contentious and full of life,"[15] while another remarks that "talk in our house was a continuum sensitive at all points of past and present and tirelessly harking back and readjusting itself, as if seeking some state of equilibrium finally free of irritation."[16] But the homelife portrayed in the Olinger works can be viewed only as highly erratic and disorienting, especially for sensitive adolescents attempting to develop mature emotional and psychological responses. Surely the tumult and uproar experienced in their formative years contribute heavily to the problems encountered by the Olinger protagonists in later life, especially with regard to their attitudes toward male-female relationships.

Despite the often idyllic tone with which the Olinger childhood and adolescence are described, the experience has obviously left certain scars. Just as Roth's Portnoy, Wallach, et al., suffer the consequences of family turbulence, Updike's protagonists are often beset by confusions that have resulted from early disruptions. If Portnoy terms his mother "The Most Unforgettable Character I've Met," certainly the Olinger mother is just as central to the Updike protagonists' life. In addition, there are certain parallels between the Rothian father figure (the self-sacrificing Jack Portnoy, in particular) and the similarly tragicomic Olinger father. In the work of both writers, ambivalent feelings toward the parents lead to difficulties for the protagonists.

In addition to stories such as "Flight" and "Pigeon Feathers," Updike has written two novels that focus specifically on Olinger and these problematic family relationships: *The Cen-*

taur, which is set in the past and concerns the father; and *Of the Farm,* which is set in the present and concerns the mother. The former novel, which won the National Book Award despite mixed reviews, is by far the fullest treatment of Updike's Olinger material. *The Centaur* presents in great detail the highly autobiographical family situation already familiar to the informed reader: the family (in this case named Caldwell) owns a farm in Firetown, just outside Olinger, having moved from the latter location after repurchasing the farm (which had originally been in the mother's family). As in the other Olinger works, however, the schoolteacher father and the young son regret having left Olinger, and the purchase of the farm has been engineered almost entirely by the mother. A strong-willed romantic, Cassie Caldwell believes that living close to the earth constitutes an affirmation of life. But George Caldwell, her husband, has quite opposite feelings, and maintains that farm life reminds him only of death, a topic seldom far from his mind.

As the story unfolds, it becomes quite obvious that Caldwell has sacrificed his personal happiness for what he believes to be the good of the family, thus becoming a hero in the eyes of his son, the narrator. The book is, in fact, Peter's celebration of his father. But again, the family situation is one of chaotic upheaval, an endless round of squabbles, misunderstandings, misdirected and misapprehended gestures. Although Peter insists that "our life together, for all its mutual frustration . . . was good. We moved, somehow, on a firm stage, resonant with metaphor" (p. 70), the only truly metaphorical significance of the events in question derives from Peter's mode of narration, a blend of perspectives that incorporates the Chiron myth into the story of George Caldwell. And the insertion of mythic elements tends, by contrast, to underscore the depressing pettiness of the Caldwells' family

life, a dreary, quarrelsome charade rendered all the more unpleasant by "haste and improvidence" (p. 273). Caldwell ultimately emerges as heroic because for Peter's sake he altruis-
tically resigns himself to an unrewarding existence. A "death
in life" is more harrowing, perhaps, than a literal demise.
And what Caldwell knowingly chooses is to continue along
with his humdrum, unsatisfying existence, for the sake of his
son and the other family members. When Updike writes
"Chiron accepted death" (p. 299), this is what he means. As
Updike has explained, "I must repeat that I didn't mean
Caldwell to die in *The Centaur;* he dies in the sense of living, of
going back to work, of being a shelter for his son."[17] The
problem, of course, is that Peter knows this and obviously
carries the knowledge as a heavy encumbrance.

It is hardly surprising that the adult Peter, even as he narrates, indicates that his life has not unfolded to his satisfaction. Now a painter, he fears that his art has come to nothing
and that his present life is unworthy of his father's sacrifice.
"Was it for this that my father gave up his life?" (p. 270), he
asks himself, and the note of recrimination is clearly sound-
ed. But in view of his childhood and adolescence, it is no
wonder that his adulthood is a disappointment. If the several
days covered in the novel are representative (and the implication is that they are), Peter's teen-age years have been bur-
dened by an entirely disproportionate measure of responsibility, and his parents have failed to provide adequate role
models, his father's selflessness notwithstanding. With regard to male-female relationships especially, Peter inadvertently reveals a rather shallow and artificial value system. His
offhanded references to his sleeping lover, for example, are
childishly sentimental. He confesses that their life together is
characterized by a "rather wistful half-Freudian half-Orien-
tal sex mysticism" (p. 270), and there is evidence that it

amounts to little more. Peter seems to have a tenuous grasp on the complexities of interpersonal attachment, and there is even a hint that he is attracted to the woman simply because she is black. It is significant also that Peter addresses his long retrospective narrative to the woman while she is asleep, a detail that suggests that true communication is not customary in their relationship.

Of course, the great bulk of the narrative is grounded in the past, and the scenes involving the adult Peter and the lover constitute only a tiny percentage of the book. As a fuller exploration of the relationship between the narrator's past and present, *Of the Farm,* though much shorter than *The Centaur* and constituting in a sense a coda to it (and to the other Olinger works), is far more explicit, and warrants extended commentary at this point, for it integrates Updike's family and marriage themes to a degree unequalled anywhere else in his canon.

The basic elements of the narrative situation are familiar. Although the family name is now Robinson and a few other minor details have once again been changed, *Of the Farm* is another installment of Updike's Olinger saga, and the initiated soon recognize the surroundings: Schoelkopf's neighboring property, Potteiger's store, nearby Galilee, Olinger, and the Firetown farm itself. There is, however, one very major difference between this and Updike's previous Olinger stories; although like the others it is a first person narrative told by the son of the family, it is set in the here and now, rather than in the nostalgic past of the narrator's boyhood. Accordingly, the tone of fond reminiscence that occasionally sentimentalizes the earlier Olinger fictions is totally absent, clearing the way for a more searching treatment of the material. The long-suffering father is now dead, the mother is elderly and nearing death, and Joey, the son, is twice married, living

in New York City. The occasion of the story is a visit that Joey
and his new wife and her young son make to the farm.

Like Lillian Dow of "Flight," Elsie Kern of "Pigeon
Feathers," and Cassie Caldwell of *The Centaur,* the complex
Mrs. Robinson does not love easily or simply. The weekend
visit is as much an existential confrontation as a family gathering, and abounds with meanings and ramifications that
carry far beyond the events of the moment. Although quite
short and involving very little dramatic action, *Of the Farm* is,
as one critic says, "the most irreducible"[18] of Updike's
works, for here the multiple strands of the Olinger chronicle
are woven tightly together in an arresting tapestry that illustrates a good many of Updike's most basic thematic preoccupations, particularly with regard to the complex interactions
that take place within families.

Joey Robinson is at a crucial point in his life and is attempting to understand his situation. Like Roth's protagonists, and like Updike's Harry Angstrom, he seeks to reconcile the often conflicting demands placed upon him by
himself and others. Since he is so very close to these others—
his two wives, his children, his dead father, his mother—the
task is difficult. For example, he is quite vulnerable to his
mother's judgments; although resentful of the strange power
that she has over him, he cannot seem to escape it. At one
point he cries, "I'm thirty-five and I've been through hell
and I don't see why that old lady has to have such a hold over
me. It's ridiculous. It's degrading" (p. 45). We are reminded
of Alexander Portnoy's allegation that "a Jewish man with
parents alive is a fifteen-year-old boy, and will remain a fifteen-year-old boy till *they die!* . . . . Did I say fifteen? Excuse
me, I meant ten! I meant five! I meant zero! A Jewish man
with his parents alive is half the time a helpless *infant!* Listen,
come to my aid, will you—and quick! Spring me from this

role I play of the smothered son in the Jewish joke! Because it's beginning to pall a little, at thirty-three!" (p. 111)

The memory of Joey's father is also a burden, and one suspects that much of Joey's impetuosity (e.g., his leaving his first wife) is an unconscious attempt to avoid repeating the father's mistakes. Although Joey rejects it as an oversimplification, Peggy's assessment of the father seems accurate, especially in view of the other Olinger works: "Peggy's idea, . . . a detailed indictment of a past that had touched her only through my hands, was that my mother had undervalued and destroyed my father, had been inadequately a 'woman' to him, had brought him to a farm which was in fact her giant lover, and had thus warped the sense of the masculine within me, her son." (p. 134)

Certainly the farm itself plays a central role in the novel, representing many things; most obviously, it is a symbol of a vanishing way of life to which the mother clings, and to which she has sacrificed her husband. For Joey, then, the farm is at the root of his identity crisis. Because of his mother's dominance, he is unsure of his sexuality and therefore of himself. Through Peggy, however, he experiences a half-unconscious epiphany by which he reaches new understanding. This moment of insight occurs while Joey is mowing the field. At one point, Joey refers to his wife as his "demesne" (p. 33), and later describes her in other terms that evoke images of the outdoors: "terrain . . . landscapes. . . . sky" (pp. 46–47). The act of mowing the field becomes aligned with the act of sexual intercourse, and this implied correspondence is plainly elicited in the highly sexual flavor of the mowing scenes:

My mother's method, when she mowed, was to embrace the field, tracing its borders and then on a slow square spiral closing in until one small central patch was left, a triangle of standing grass or an hour glass that became two triangles before vanishing. Mine was to slice, in one ecstatic straight thrust, up the middle. . . . I, rocked back and forth on the iron seat shaped like a woman's hips, alone in nature, as hidden under the glaring sky as at midnight, excited by destruction, weightless, discovered in myself a swelling which I idly permitted to stand, thinking of Peggy. My wife is a field. (pp. 58–59)

These passages describing the mowing are crucial to an understanding of the insight that Joey acquires by the end of the novel. We know that the mother was the dominant figure in her marriage, and that she assumed the male role in relation to the farm. Joey says that his father "never farmed," to which his mother adds, "he bought me a tractor and let me keep the fields mowed" (p. 24). On four separate occasions, Joey alludes to having witnessed his mother outrun his father (pp. 7, 55, 97, and 166), and several other times the mother is depicted in a "masculine" role. In her first appearance in the novel, for example, she is wearing "a man's wool sweater" (p. 8) and she is said to have a "squarish hand, short-fingered and worn like a man's" (p. 173).

The mowing scenes symbolize Joey's conscious attempt to overcome his mother's domination and affirm his own individuality. These scenes are invested with a great deal of oedipal significance, as Joey shaves with his father's razor, dons his father's pants, and generally assumes the patriarchal role. This is further reinforced when, during the second stage of the mowing, Joey requests a hat. "All I need is a hat of Daddy's," he says, to which the mother replies, "He never wore a hat. I'm surprised you've forgotten" (p. 91). That Joey eventually wears a hat of his mother's signifies that he has assumed the traditionally masculine managerial role that the mother had appropriated from the father. Updike's implication seems to be that things are now as they should be: in line with the young minister's sermon, in which the proper role of women is defined as subordinate, complementary and sub-missive, that of a "help meet" (p. 150).

Whether or not we agree with such a conventionally sexist position, Updike clearly intends for the mowing scenes and those that follow to suggest that Joey Robinson finds recon-ciliation only after symbolically rejecting female dominance and adopting a traditionally assertive male role. This idea is underscored once again when, as Joey concludes his mow-ing, he is bathed in rainfall (a positive symbol of regenera-tion), signifying that the very elements are approving his ef-forts; as if in assent, the mother grants that Joey has done a "man-sized" (p. 173) job. Indeed, the seizure that the moth-er experiences near the end of the novel, and which she attri-butes to the idea that "her arteries couldn't take so much happiness" (p. 172), may in fact be partly a result of the sud-den realization that although her son is now beyond her con-trol, with his own life to lead, he is finally a "man."

Of course, such a neat schematization does violence to the book's subtlety, and the final resolution is tentative and deli-cate. Indeed, this is the book's primary strength. Although the characters have come to recognize the need for a greater degree of flexibility in their dealings with one another, the fundamental tensions remain. Updike describes *Of the Farm* as a novel of "moral readjustment"[19] concerning "the mutu-al forgiveness of mother and son, the acceptance each of the other's guilt."[20] But, as in life, the situation is not wholly re-solved, nor can it be. As in Roth's *Letting Go*, the solutions achieved are at best partial, for the nature of the dilemmas defies total resolution. Although both Roth and Updike have occasionally been assailed because of the somewhat inconclu-sive endings of their works, in *Letting Go* and *Of the Farm* the tentative attitudes in which the characters are left reveal that these authors are in control of their material, for any other type of conclusion would constitute a falsification. Such novels reflect the authors' great skill at examining the various conflicts that can exist within families, but they also reveal a wise authorial deference to the fact that family relationships are seldom amenable to pat, formulaic reduction.

4

Sons and Lovers: Romantic Involvement and Personal Morality in Roth and Updike

THE LARGE ISSUE of personal moral responsibility and guilt is of great interest to Philip Roth and John Updike, featuring centrally in practically everything they have written. It is integral to the themes already discussed— ethnic identity and family interactions—but it finds expression in another area of shared emphasis as well: love and marriage. Both writers are dominantly concerned with human sexuality and its attendant complexities, specifically as manifested in romantic relationships. Roth's and Updike's lovers seem always to be stymied by a fundamental conflict involving the demands of the self versus one's obligations to others, and are frequently beset by feelings of inadequacy and guilt because of their failure to understand or balance this basic opposition.

In Roth's earliest works (the *Goodbye, Columbus* novella and short stories) and in his most recent (the "Zuckerman" novels), the love-marriage theme is obviously crucial. The mutually exploitive "summer romance" between Neil Klugman and Brenda Patimkin in the *Goodbye, Columbus* novella serves as a context wherein Roth explores several larger themes. But the principals' sexual relationship becomes an important consideration in its own right, permitting Roth to comment trenchantly upon the destructive consequences of romantic self-delusion. Two of the five *Goodbye, Columbus* short stories focus on married characters whose difficulties are directly related to their unsatisfactory marital relationships: the aging title character in "Epstein" is mired in the final throes of a disappointing union, and the marriage depicted in "Eli, the Fanatic" contributes heavily to the protagonist's problems. In *The Ghost Writer,* young Nathan Zuckerman is shocked by the acrimonious discord of his mentor's homelife, while the mature Nathan of *Zuckerman Unbound* and *The Anatomy Lesson* has himself experienced a series of unsuccessful marriages and romances. As we have seen, such predicaments feature prominently in Roth's other works as well, particularly so in *Letting Go, When She Was Good,* and *Portnoy's Complaint.*

Indeed, *Portnoy's Complaint* can be viewed as the first volume in a Rothian "Trilogy of Desire" also including *My Life as a Man* and *The Professor of Desire.* These novels, perhaps more emphatically than any others in his canon, reflect Roth's ongoing preoccupation with, in his own words, "the struggle to accommodate warring (or, at least, contending) impulses and desires, to negotiate some kind of inner peace or balance of power, or perhaps just to maintain hostilities at a low destructive level, between the ethical and social yearnings and the . . . singular lusts of the flesh and its pleasures. The measured self vs. the insatiable self. The accommodating self vs. the ravenous self."[1] In *Portnoy's Complaint,* the major social issues of ethnic identity, cultural assimilation, and family tensions are clearly present, and function as basic themes. But their primary purpose is to provide a setting in which to examine Portnoy's sexuality. In fact, Portnoy—or his erotomania—dominates the social content and overshadows it (although Portnoy believes the opposite to be true). He thereby engages our attention, becoming an extreme but recognizable embodiment of the universal implacability of the flesh.

The same might be said of the wife-hating Peter Tarnopol in *My Life as a Man,* except that the stridency of his narration renders him finally boring rather than interesting. While somewhat less physically explicit than *Portnoy's Complaint, My Life as a Man* is even more insistent in delineating "the battle of the sexes." Yet *My Life as a Man* is not Roth's most effective treatment of the love-marriage theme. The novel contains several finely wrought sections ("Salad Days," for example, is an impressive performance), but many of the insights tend to slip out of focus, overpowered by the sheer redundancy of their dissection and the cloyingly self-justifying tone of the delivery. Tarnopol's story is actually Roth's vehement gesture of retribution toward his own late wife, and the personal animus motivating the work finally undermines it. An instructive comparison could be made, in fact, between *My Life as a Man* and Updike's similarly autobiographical "divorce" stories in the *Problems* collection. In Updike's stories, the particular provides access to the universal, for he has been able to step back from his own experience, using it as a source for fiction rather than for obsessive self-flagellation.

Of course, *My Life as a Man* is not mere transcription. Much constructive fabrication surrounds this treatment of Roth's marriage, and the book's whole conception is quite consciously "literary," particularly with regard to form. Perhaps the most immediately noticeable of the novel's various interesting features is its reflexive structure, an experimental format that constitutes a variation on the *Künstlerroman.* What makes the book somewhat unusual—although not unique—

is that it extends the parameters of that genre to become not just a novel about a fictional artist, but, ostensibly, a collection of that author's work. The first section, "Useful Fictions," consists of two short stories ("Salad Days" and "Courting Disaster") supposedly written by Tarnopol.

My Life as a Man is structurally challenging then, and addresses significant issues. Moreover, it may well have been the book that Roth "had to" write at that particular point in his life. Nevertheless, the novel is disappointing, primarily because the narrator's splenetic ravings are too unrelieved. Roth practically grants this, as he has Tarnopol quoting Flaubert's letter to his mistress, Louise Colet, concerning her poetic attack on Alfred de Musset: "You wrote with a personal emotion that distorted your outlook and made it impossible to keep before your eyes the fundamental principles that must underlie any imaginative composition. . . . You have turned art into an outlet for passion, a kind of chamberpot to catch an overflow. It smells bad; it smells of hate!"[2] Tarnopol admits that "all I can do with my story is tell it. And tell it. And tell it. And *that's* the truth" (p. 231). But this is a truth in which the reader soon loses interest. Although the events of Tarnopol's tumultuous life are potentially quite absorbing, Roth's inability—or unwillingness—to treat his intensely personal subject matter somewhat more dispassionately results in a narrator-protagonist whose struggles with the eros-agape and self-others conflicts soon seem to lose significance, for he appears to wallow in, and almost to relish, defeat.

This is the most immediately recognizable difference between Tarnopol and Portnoy, a contrast that sharply reveals the latter's greater substance as a fictional creation: Portnoy is engaging in a way that Tarnopol never is. Of course, this is largely because Portnoy is immensely entertaining, and because his egocentricity is continually undercut by his own sense of comic self-deflation. Hence he remains somehow appealing, even at his most vile. No matter how desperate his plight becomes, he never loses his theatrical impulse or his awareness that he is dramatizing himself. There is something redeeming about this. Despite the seriousness of Portnoy's neuroses—as typified by his self-hatred—he possesses throughout, even in the catastrophic scenes in Israel with Naomi, a certain manic appeal. He has, to coin a phrase, an "immoral fiber" that Tarnopol lacks, which endears him to us in spite of his many shortcomings. As a consequence, we tend to take more seriously his attempts to resolve the sexual conflicts that beset him.

Essentially, Portnoy's difficulty is the same as that of most of Roth's protagonists: he is unable to reconcile the opposed demands of the superego and the id. Roth's puritanical hedonists are all at war with their own dual natures, futilely striving to effect a truce between incompatible urges. Perhaps the best example is David Kepesh, protagonist of *The Professor of Desire*. This is among the most satisfying of Roth's novels because here he managed to fuse Portnoy's appeal and Tarnopol's sobriety, creating in Kepesh one of his most credible narrators. A typically urbane and sophisticated Rothian protagonist, Kepesh presents the details of his plight in a polished, controlled, and wryly amusing manner. Eschewing the caustic self-righteousness of Neil Klugman, the stuffy solemnity of Gabe Wallach, the erratic histrionism of Portnoy, and the shrill lugubriousness of Tarnopol, he states his case in a voice that is eminently suited to the book's themes. It is Roth's most convincing attempt so far to create the illusion of extemporaneous first person narration.

In *The Professor of Desire,* Roth retained all the strengths of *My Life as a Man* while avoiding that book's weaknesses. He continued to perfect not only the narrative voice, but also those other facets of fictive creation that had always been his virtues: the capacity for sharp evocations of setting through selective description and allusion, the ability to render character by means of a few deft strokes of incisive portraiture, an almost preternatural sensitivity to the distinctive qualities of realistic dialogue, and a highly developed sense of the absurd as it manifests itself in the everyday lives of his characters. Interestingly, *The Professor of Desire* largely retains *My Life as a Man's* concern with the despised spouse, but in the more recent novel Roth is always in control of his material. Therefore, this subject does not dominate the book, but simply serves as one of several that are pursued for the purpose of revealing the intricacies of the protagonist's inner workings.

In its handling of the theme of interpersonal responsibility and guilt, then, *The Professor of Desire* is the most convincing of the "Trilogy of Desire" novels, the one broadest in its applications. Kepesh's difficulties are akin to those of Portnoy or Tarnopol, but his particular case is more persuasively delineated and more convincingly stated than those others, because it is presented with so much more artistic detachment and reserve. All aspects of the book neatly coalesce to create a fully rounded picture of Kepesh's personality.

Dr. Klinger (who plays Spielvogel to Kepesh's Portnoy) says that for Kepesh, "moral delinquency has its fascination" (p. 102). This is obvious even at the outset of the novel, as Kepesh devotes the opening pages to a celebration of Herbie Bratasky, a childhood hero who had been "social director, bandleader, crooner, comic, and m.c." (p. 3) of the Catskills resort hotel run by young Kepesh's parents. What most fascinates David about Herbie is that, in short, he is "crazy enough for anything—that's his whole *act*" (p. 5). For example, he can vocally imitate the entire range of bathroom noises "ranging from the faintest springtime sough to the twenty-one-gun salute—with which mankind emits its gases. . . . he can also 'do diarrhea'" (pp. 6–7). That such talents should intrigue a school aged child is not surprising, but Kepesh's admiration for Herbie's mimetic virtuosity is simply the first in a series of adulatory attachments that throughout his life will reveal his split personality: the wild, libidinous, self-indulgent side vs. the serious, responsible, scholarly component. In college, for example, Kepesh explains the apparent dichotomy between his "high grades and . . . base desires" by quoting Byron—"Studious by day, dissolute by night" (p. 17). Later, as an academic, Kepesh aligns himself with poet-in-residence Ralph Baumgarten, a notorious Lothario whose poetry and private life alike reveal that "for him flagrance appears to be much of the fun" (p. 123), and finally earn him ostracism. Although he himself is outwardly sober and conventional, Kepesh is repeatedly drawn to arrantly flamboyant types such as Bratasky, Jelinek, and Baumgarten because of the repressed side of his personality, his more unseemly and lubricious—and actually dominant—aspect.

It is in Kepesh's relationships with women, though, that this tendency is most evident, and it is around these relationships that *The Professor of Desire* really revolves. As numerous critics have mentioned, women in Roth's trilogy (as in much of Updike's work) are seldom presented as fully rendered characters in their own right, but fall into three rather reductive categories determined almost exclusively by their relationships to the male protagonists.[3] Briefly stated, these classifications are as follows: the "lascivious girl" whose sexual abandon at once enthralls and unnerves the protagonist; the castrating "bitch" who seeks to master the protagonist; and the "nice girl" who, despite her obvious attractions (including a "normal" degree of sexual gusto), ultimately bores the protagonist.

In each of the "Desire" novels, there is at least one example of each type. In *Portnoy's Complaint,* for example, the "lascivious girl" appears in imaginary form as Thereal McCoy and in actuality as "The Monkey." The critic Martin Amis has pointed out that the emasculating woman in *Portnoy's Complaint* is not immediately identifiable for she appears not as one of Portnoy's lovers, but as Sophie Portnoy, the stifling *yiddishe mama.*[4] And the "nice girl" role is shared by "The Pumpkin" and "The Pilgrim." In *My Life as a Man,* Sharon Shatsky is the wanton, Maureen Johnson Tarnopol is the "ball-breaker," and Susan Seabury McCall is the "nice girl." In *The Professor of Desire,* the three categories are represented by lascivious Birgitta Svanström, emasculating Helen Baird Kepesh, and "nice girls" Elisabeth Elverskog and Claire Ovington.

In attempting to evaluate his dealings with these women, Kepesh realizes that he is blocked by a basic contradiction. He desperately yearns for sexual abandon, but whenever he embraces it (as with Birgitta and Helen) his consequent guilt feelings drive him toward *less* sensual, more conventional women (Elisabeth and Claire); ironically, he then loses interest in those women and his guilt is increased, resulting in impotence and melancholia. Helen accuses Kepesh of being a "young fogy" (p. 71) and of despising "fun" (p. 60), but really that is not his problem. Rather, the opposite is true. He is not stuffy or strait-laced, but is actually a libertine; paradoxically, he cannot accept that fact. In the final analysis, Kepesh is *too* fun oriented. Always, though, Kepesh is aware of the tension between the two sides of his personality, so that whichever aspect he is embracing at any given moment, he is never at peace. When he indulges his earthy impulses he often feels that he is in a state of "contamination" (p. 135), yet with the wholesome Claire he cannot repress the nagging feeling that there is something too "perfect" about her. In less guarded moments, when he is not deliberately trying to heed his own "better judgment," his feelings toward her are negative: "Anger; disappointment; disgust—contempt for all she does so marvelously, resentment over that little thing she will not deign to do. I see how very easily I could have no use for her. The snapshots. The lists. The mouth that will not drink my come. The curriculum-review committee. Everything" (p. 162). The problem is that for Kepesh, "'Birgitta' and 'more' are just different ways of saying the same thing," while "'Claire' and 'enough'—they, too, are one word" (p. 165), but for Kepesh "enough" is not enough. Hence he envisions a situation of hopelessness, a quandary in which there is no solution: "I am ready to think it is something about me that makes for the sadness; about how I have always failed to be what people want or expect; how I have never quite pleased anyone, including myself; how, hard as I have tried, I have seemed never quite able to be one thing or the other, and probably never will be" (p. 222).

Clearly, the novel is a serious one. In addition to Kepesh's individual dilemmas, Roth touches also on the theme of death, and even ventures—atypically—into covert political commentary, on the repression practiced against writers and intellectuals in the Iron Curtain countries. Despite these sobering concerns, however, *The Professor of Desire* is not without its upbeat elements. More than in any other of Roth's novels the bittersweet complications of deeply-felt filial love are fully explored, as Kepesh reveals his sincere and unashamed attachment to his parents. As discussed earlier, the elder Kepesh is indeed the most affectionately drawn of Roth's many fathers, and here even the "Jewish mother"—certainly a figure of derision in Roth's *Portnoy's Complaint*—emerges in a fully sympathetic light. There is abundant humor as well. But the humor in *The Professor of Desire* is seldom belittling or raucous, as in *Portnoy's Complaint;* it is gentler, more subtle, more akin to the comedic elements in Roth's "'I Always Wanted You to Admire My Fasting'; or Looking at Kafka," another of his most accomplished works.

All of this serves to create a more balanced tonal impression than in any of Roth's previous novels. It is in this sense quite mature, as it not only probes the underside of interpersonal culpability, but also celebrates the more positively reinforcing aspects of interdependency, commitment, and love. The sections that chronicle Kepesh and Claire's idyllic existence at their summer hideaway are among the most lyrical in recent fiction, creating a feeling of peaceful reconciliation reminiscent of that evoked by the closing Ludeyville passages in Bellow's *Herzog*. Indeed, Roth has publicly acknowledged his admiration for Bellow's work (in the dedication to *Reading Myself and Others* and elsewhere), and *The Professor of Desire* owes much to the older writer's influence. Generally, the more reserved, less insistent, and more considered viewpoint that Roth first evinced here (and largely retained in the "Zuckerman" novels) reminds one of Bellow's sagacious tentativeness, his poignant ambiguity. There are specific referents, as well. Kepesh's habit of vacillation followed by ill-advised choice recalls Tommy Wilhelm's in *Seize the Day*, as a comparison of the following two passages illustrates:

When he was best aware of the risks and knew a hundred reasons against going and had made himself sick with fear, he left home. This was typical of Wilhelm. After much thought and hesitation and debate he invariably took the course he had rejected innumerable times. Ten such decisions made up the history of his life.

. . . He had made up his mind not to marry his wife, but ran off and got married.[5]

Doubting and hoping then, wanting and fearing (anticipating the pleasantest sort of lively future one moment, the worst in the next), I marry Helen Baird—after, that is, nearly three full years devoted to doubting-hoping-wanting-and-fearing. . . . after an interminable vacillation. . . . I marry Helen when the weight of experience required to reach the monumental decision to give her up for good turns out to be . . . enormous (p. 66).

In addition, Kepesh's habitual cry of "I want somebody" (p. 106) echoes Henderson's almost identical "I want" in Bellow's *Henderson the Rain King*. A Bellow novel is actually mentioned when Kepesh refers to "Herzogian helplessness" (p. 157).

There is considerable humor throughout. But, as already mentioned, it is low-key as often as it is uproarious. True, certain touches are typically Rothian: Kepesh's oddball mentors (Herbie, Jelinek, and Baumgarten) provide quite a few guffaws, as do the remembered snippets of resort hotel life; the ludicrous "Wally" scenes generate more belly laughs, as a persistent homosexual harrasses the beleagured Kepesh via the apartment building intercom; and the dream sequence involving Kafka's whore is as bizarrely comical as anything in "On the Air." Generally, however, Roth's humor is noticeably subdued in this novel. The scenes toward the end, in which Kepesh's recently widowed, hyperactive father attempts to conceal his glee over the son's apparent decision to "settle down" with Claire, are exemplary. Although comic touches abound, there is also a pervasively somber undertone that consistently informs the text, creating an unmistakably tragicomic dimension. This, too, is Bellovian.

Ultimately, *The Professor of Desire* is one of Roth's best books because it is among his most intelligent. The intricacies of in-

terpersonal responsibility and guilt are never oversimplified
(as they sometimes are elsewhere in his corpus), mainly because Roth is more reluctant here to pass moral judgments.
Even where guilt is clearly proven, the blame is withheld.
Roth seems to suggest that Kepesh's problems are not the
fault of his or anyone else's shortcomings, but are a condition
of life itself. Even the rigidly "proper" Arthur Schonbrunn,
Kepesh's stuffy department chairperson, reveals by his attempts to seduce Kepesh's beautiful wife, Helen, that he too
has his hedonistic, irresponsible aspect. The obvious implication is that everyone does, and that this is what makes "normal" living—with its restraints, strictures, and responsibilities—frustrating and ultimately unsatisfying. To this
degree, Kepesh is Everyman, except that his situation is exaggerated, as is usual in Roth's fiction. Kepesh's frustrations
are not unlike those depicted in the Chekhov stories to which
he alludes:

I return to Chekhov's fiction nightly, listening for the anguished cry
of the trapped and miserable socialized being, the well-bred wives
who during dinner with guests wonder "Why do I smile and lie?",
and the husbands, seemingly settled and secure, who are "full of
conventional truth and conventional deception." Simultaneously I
am watching how Chekhov, simply and clearly, though not so piti-
lessly as Flaubert, reveals the humiliations and failures—worst of
all, the destructive power—of those who seek a way *out* of the pervasive boredom and the stifling despair, out of the painful marital situations and the endemic social falsity, into what they take to be a vibrant and desirable life. (p. 156)

Certainly, this is the purpose of the numerous literary references that appear so often in the text: to reinforce and lend
authority to the novel's basic suppositions. This device is entirely appropriate, for Kepesh, as a university professor of literature, would be apt to think in such terms.

The many mentions of Chekhov, Kafka, Dostoevsky, Flaubert, Mann, Tolstoy, and others serve to support the novel's basic assertion that, as one of Kepesh's students writes on her final examination, "we are born innocent, we suffer terrible disillusionment before we can gain knowledge, and then we fear death—and we are granted only fragmentary happiness to offset the pain" (p. 94). As Kepesh envisions it, the disillusionment, fear, and consequent anguish are largely the result of people's inability to perceive how they stand in relation to themselves and to their antithetical moralistic and prurient urges. And of course, this is by implication related to the whole larger issue of interpersonal relationships. At one point, Kepesh asks himself why there seems to be no American writer able to rival Colette in handling these realities:

I have been wondering if there has ever been in America a novelist with a point of view toward the taking and giving of pleasure even vaguely resembling Colette's, an American writer, man or woman, stirred as deeply as she is by scent and warmth and color, someone as sympathetic to the range of the body's urgings, as attuned to the world's every sensuous offering, a connoisseur of the finest gradations of amorous feeling, who is nonetheless immune to fanaticism of any sort, except, as with Colette, a fanatical devotion to the self's honorable survival (pp. 201-2).

A moment later, Kepesh suggests that perhaps it is Updike who comes closest. And, of course, this estimate is quite correct. Updike's protagonists strive always for self-realization, and do so in a highly antinomian manner, often disregarding all but their own hearts' needs. Updike seems to be suggesting two things by this: that such behavior reflects our communal loss of moral sensitivity, but that—given this loss—a devotion to individual survival at any price may be an appropriate and fitting commitment. Updike himself has commented on the relationship between the individual and society in his fiction: "I see each book as a picturing of actual tensions, conflicts, and awkward spots in our private and social lives. My books feed, I suppose, on some kind of perverse relish in the fact that there are insolvable problems. . . . There is no way to reconcile . . . individual wants to the very real need of any society to set strict limits and to confine its members."[6]

Sometimes, as in the case of the Reverend Mr. Marshfield of *A Month of Sundays,* Jerry Conant of *Marry Me,* or Piet Hanema of *Couples,* the protagonist evinces an aggressively single-minded preoccupation with self. Of course, there are certain problems with this. Marshfield and Conant, for example, are deeply flawed personalities, and are presented as such. Hence their assertive egotism seems repellent rather than courageous. With Piet Hanema, the "hero's" intended superiority is apparent but barely credible, predicated on no real evidence other than a few heavy-handed symbols or some other contrivance, such as Hanema's "cruciform blazon of amber hair" (p. 7) meant to connote the religious dimension of his personality. Updike has said that *Couples* is "not about sex really: it's about sex as the emergent religion, as the only thing left. I don't present the people in the book as a set of villains: I see them as people caught in a historical moment."[7] Clearly, the incessant sexual activity that so permeates *Couples, Marry Me,* and *A Month of Sundays* is on one level metaphoric. Promiscuity, Updike implies, is an index of social instability; and Freddy Thorne, the sinister dentist in *Couples,* maintains that the spouse swappers constitute a "magic circle of heads to keep the night out," in effect, "a church" (p. 7), the only sort of church possible in "one of those dark ages that visits mankind between millenia, between the death and rebirth of gods, when there is nothing to steer by but sex and stoicism and the stars" (p. 372).

In *A Month of Sundays,* the Reverend Mr. Marshfield delivers sermons in which adultery is presented almost as a sacrament, an avenue to spiritual rebirth. Piet Hanema and Jerry Conant are churchgoers, but they too attempt to transform traditional religious belief into a purely secular and self-indulgent sensuality. In the heavily symbolic conclusion of *Couples,* the Tarbox Congregationalist church is consumed by fire, having been struck in biblical fashion by "God's own lightning" (p. 441), and only the penny-eyed metal weathercock (certainly a token of both pagan sexuality and empty materialism) is salvaged: "three stiff delegates of the church accepted the old emblem and posed for photographs absurdly, cradling the piece of tin between them; the man on Pedrick's right had hairy ears, the one on the left was a jeweler. The swarming children encircled them and touched the dull metal. The sky above was empty but for two parallel jet trails" (p. 457). Updike's implication here is plain: contemporary America has turned to false gods that are but a poor substitute for conventional belief and practice; in *Marry Me* and *A Month of Sundays,* a similar moral emerges. Unfortunately, however, each of the three novels is deeply flawed.

Updike's underlying conceptions in these "suburban" fictions are quite sound, but throughout there is a thinness of characterization that seriously undermines the novels' effectiveness. In *Couples,* for example, it is not only hard to experience the characters as real, it is often difficult even to tell them apart. That the mate-trading Applebys and Smiths are referred to as the "Applesmiths" by the other couples (just as the Saltzes and the Constantines become the "Saltines") is reflective of the fact that individuals in this book tend to blur and merge, as one couple becomes indistinguishable from another. Granted, several critics have suggested that this is intentional on Updike's part, in order to convey the adulterers' lack of identity. But whether intended or not, the overall effect is damaging. Aside from the grotesque, adrogynous Thorne, only Hanema emerges with any clarity; and even he is superficially drawn, becoming more a symbol of obsolete virtues and "impossible ideals" (p. 449) than a fully realized creation. Characters such as Hanema, Conant, and Marshfield are two-dimensional. Despite the quasi-religious context in which their doings are presented, there is something too simplistic about their self-righteousness, something too automatic about their self-gratification. Far more realistic are those more complex Updikean protagonists who opt for self reluctantly, only after careful and soul-wrenching consideration of the consequences of their actions. Richard Maple of the "Maples" stories is one example, and the many other (highly autobiographical) divorced or nearly divorced men of the *Problems* collection share his questioning tentativeness. Updike's alienated antiheros are more persuasive when they are presented this way, as perplexed, wounded seekers rather than as blithely self-indulgent egotists.

Harry Angstrom is the quintessential Updikean protagonist. Harry is a very balanced character whose portrayal avoids the excesses of Marshfield's, Conant's, or Hanema's—or, for that matter, of the contrastingly saintly George Caldwell's in *The Centaur*. As Charles Thomas Samuels phrases it, Harry Angstrom is "Updike's most magnanimous blend of toughness and compassion. . . . [He is] someone whose value is neither exaggerated nor unconvincing."[8] I am referring now to the Harry of *Rabbit, Run* rather than to his later incarnations in *Rabbit Redux* and *Rabbit Is Rich*, for in the more recent books Harry is for the most part quite passive, more acted upon than acting. Certainly Harry's passivity is central to the sequels' intentions, while in *Rabbit, Run* he assumes a vitally active role, pitting his nearly transcendentalist faith in self-reliance, the oversoul, and individual primacy against the leveling influences of societal norms and conventions. Updike has said, in fact, that he wrote *Rabbit, Run* "just to say that there is no solution. It is a novel about the bouncing, the oscillating back and forth between these two kinds of urgencies."[9] Indeed, *Rabbit, Run* remains Updike's most totally successful book, principally because the character of Harry best embodies the author's various themes: religion and the lost past, parental relationships, marriage, and sexuality and personal accountability. Moreover, his amorality is not only a feature of his own predicament, but can also be seen as an index of national corruption as well.

Tony Tanner asserts that

there is an abiding dream in American literature that an unpatterned, unconditioned life is possible, in which your movements and stillnesses, choices and repudiations are all your own; and that there is also an abiding American dread that someone else is patterning your life, that there are all sorts of invisible plots afoot to rob you of your autonomy of thought and action, that conditioning is ubiquitous. The problematic and ambiguous relationship of the self to patterns of all kinds . . . is an obsession among . . . American writers.[10]

Surely this is true; the image of the embattled individual resisting regimentation and imposed limitations is among the most dominant and longstanding American literary conceptions. From classical American literature, characters such as Natty Bumppo and Huck Finn come immediately to mind as examples, and from more recent books Bellow's Augie

March, Salinger's Holden Caulfield, Kesey's McMurphy, and Heller's Yossarian are but a few that suggest themselves.

This is the tradition that Updike works within in *Rabbit, Run* where protagonist Harry Angstrom, like these other characters, literally takes flight. He does so for much the same reason: to assert the primacy of the individual. The aspect of Harry's running that emerges most plainly is its potential for affording spiritual liberation. Nowhere is this more evident than in the conclusion of the novel: "His hands lift of their own and he feels the wind on his ears . . . his heels hitting heavily on the pavement at first but with an effortless gathering out of a kind of sweet panic growing lighter and quicker and quieter, he runs. Ah: runs. Runs" (pp. 306–7).

Throughout the novel, Harry's impulsive physicality, of which the running is but one expression, serves as an index of his inner strength. In an ironic inversion of the traditional Christian conception of a body-soul dichotomy, Updike affirms the spiritual through the physical. Harry's quest for higher meaning, the "something that wants me to find it" (p. 127), is channeled mostly through physical avenues: sport, sexuality, and Harry's highly developed sensory acuity. To Harry, "everything seems unreal that is outside of his sensations" (p. 197). Yet, for all his earthliness, Harry's motivations are essentially religious. More than anyone else in the novel, he believes in that "thing behind everything" (p. 280), and his every action is an attempt to discover it and to apprehend it. Although Harry is by no means knowledgeable in formal theology, he possesses an intrinsic awareness of the possibility of transcendence. This intuitive spirituality sets Harry apart and renders his seemingly irresponsible behavior meaningful.

Ironically, however, there is also something naïvely child-like about Harry's belief. Indeed, one scholar has written a

book-length study of *Rabbit, Run*, entitled *Puer Aeternus*, which
attempts to show the full extent of this aspect of Harry's characterization.[11] For one thing, Harry is unable to conceptual-
ize his faith—or to verbalize it—except in the most rudimen-
tary terms. Moreover, he is disturbedly aware, as a child
might be, that the nature and intensity of his belief are somehow at variance with the popular consensus. In his own way
Harry is curiously innocent. He feels that he is "outside
. . . all America" (p. 33) as he steadfastly resists all evidence
of the void: "He hates all the people on the street in dirty everyday clothes, advertising their belief that the world arches
over a pit, that death is final, that the wandering thread of his
feelings leads nowhere. Correspondingly he loves the ones
dressed for church; the pressed business suits of portly men
give substance and respectability to his furtive sensations of
the invisible" (pp. 234–35).

Harry desperately wants to believe in "the sky as the
source of all things" (p. 280), and this in large part is what his
lover Ruth alludes to when she says that she admires Harry
because he hasn't "given up" and in his "stupid way" is
"still fighting" (p. 91). Unlike the majority, Harry is never
disillusioned, and clings to his own convictions tenaciously.
Harry steadfastly withstands what he feels to be the corrupting influence of popular opinion, which seems to him to ne-
gate the transcendent. Frustrated by the doubt and agnosti-
cism that he finds in those around him—especially in the
Reverend Mr. Eccles—he asks himself, "Why did they teach
you such things if no one believed them?" (pp. 112–13). Yet,
as David Galloway stresses, his own faith remains firm:

His absolute devotion to a quest for meaning dictates his absolute
aloneness in a society which knows nothing of meaning. To these
people he is not only an enigma, but he is destructive. . . . Like

Heller's *Catch-22, Rabbit, Run* emphasizes that man is victimized by life itself, and it remains for him to seek salvation alone—even when that means a rejection of human solidarity. . . . Rabbit Angstrom does demand confirmation of a voice which calls to man and asks him to make life meaningful. Heroes like Rabbit reject formal Christianity because it is not religious enough. What they seek is not the consoling reinforcement of dogma or ritual but some transcendent inner vision of truth. . . . Despite its secular origins there is something holy in such austere dedication to truth. Rabbit remains true to a standard of good by which he attempts to live, and the intensity of his loyalty to this standard can only be described as "religious."[12]

Quite clearly, and despite numerous critics' claims to the contrary, Updike wishes the reader to see in Rabbit a purity of response that is almost prelapsarian in its simplicity. This, of course, is the whole purpose of the Edenic pastoral interlude during which Harry serves as gardener for old Mrs. Smith of symbolically-named Appleboro. Actually, Harry's zest for life and his seemingly heretical self-determinism are related, stemming from a basis of belief that is more conventional than that of anyone else in the novel. When Eccles admonishes Harry that his faith is too literal, or when his ex-coach, Tothero, advises him that "right and wrong aren't dropped from the sky. We. We make them" (p. 279), the greater validity of Harry's own position becomes unmistakable.

Harry's stalwart adherence to deeply rooted, traditionally God-centered faith—simplistic and childlike as it is—is consistent with the teachings of Kierkegaard and Karl Barth, two of Updike's acknowledged mentors. Both believe that individual religious feeling must be grounded in empirical truth, and both stress the need for acknowledging the existence of Deity. Updike has said, in paraphrase of Barth, that "there is no help from within—without the supernatural the natural is a pit of horror. . . . all problems are basically insoluble and . . . faith is a leap out of total despair."[13] Harry Angstrom makes that leap.

In so doing, however, Harry abrogates practically all of his interpersonal responsibilities. This is what so complicates his case, and accounts for the fact that so many literary critics have written him off as a heedless, uncaring scoundrel. He abandons his pregnant wife and young son, takes refuge with a sometimes-prostitute, returns to his wife only to leave her again after placing unreasonable demands on her (thereby becoming the indirect cause of her accidentally drowning their new baby), creates an absurd disturbance at the infant's funeral, and returns to the prostitute, only to leave her upon finding that she too has become pregnant by him. Hardly the itinerary of a saint! Not surprisingly, various other characters in the novel assail Harry's selfish tendencies. Predictably, his mother-in-law asserts that "he doesn't care who he hurts or how much" (p. 154), and even the Reverend Mr. Eccles, who usually tends to defend Harry, at one point admonishes him, "You're monstrously selfish. You're a coward. You don't care about right and wrong; you worship nothing except your own worst instincts" (p. 133).

Such accusations hardly seem unjustified when we consider not only Harry's actions, but also certain of his comments. Despite his ethereal aspect, he often reveals a seemingly callous disregard for anyone but himself. "If you're telling me I'm not mature," he says to Eccles, "that's one thing I don't cry over since as far as I can make out it's the same thing as being dead" (p. 106). Elsewhere, with "an idle remote smugness," he tells Ruth that "if you have the guts to be yourself, other people'll pay your price" (p. 149). And when Janice suggests that he is incapable of understanding how she feels, he replies, "I can. I can but I don't want to, it's not the thing, the thing is how *I* feel. And I feel like getting out" (p. 248).

Clearly, Rabbit's "split personality" is Updike's way of recognizing that few persons or situations can be neatly labeled as good or bad, moral or immoral, right or wrong. Updike has said, "I don't wish my fiction to be any clearer than life,"[14] and in this novel especially there are two sides to every moral question. "My work says 'yes, but,'" Updike explains; "Yes, in *Rabbit, Run,* to our inner urgent whispers, but—the social fabric collapses murderously."[15] Central to this paradox is the epigraph that Updike has chosen from Pascal's *Pensées:* "The motions of Grace, the hardness of the heart; external circumstances." Although much has been written in the attempt to relate the epigraph to the concerns expressed in the novel, Clinton Burhans, Jr.'s analysis is by far the most cogent:

The terms of the epigraph balance on the semicolon; "the motions of Grace" and "the hardness of the heart" are two equal parts of a single term itself equal in grammatical value to "external circumstances." In other words, man's behavior and its related internal motivations are inseparable from and influenced by his external conditions. Whether he responds to "the motions of Grace" or to "the hardness of the heart" will depend substantially on the nature of the milieu in which he grows and functions. In the epigraph, too, then, Updike seems to point thematically to the portrayal of a representative man's potentialities and through him to a study of the culture which shapes them.[16]

Harry's vacillation between hardheartedness and what Ruth terms his "mildness" (p. 146) is an adjunct of his entrapment in the snares of contemporary absurdity. Updike appears to exonerate Harry by suggesting that his irresponsibility reflects a larger, national confusion. Harry's shortcomings are less reprehensible than they seem, Updike implies, because Harry's entire milieu is so compromised. Once again Updike has created a character whose disaffiliation derives not only from that one character's anxieties, but from the failure of desacralized modern life to provide stable referents. Harry is as he is because—to a great extent—"external circumstances" have made him so: "the pathos of Rabbit Angstrom arises from the irredeemable waste of his alternate possibilities; and the significance of his story is the sobering point of view it provides on a civilization whose institutions and values are apparently disintegrating, a civilization losing the power to civilize. . . . the ultimate loss is frighteningly more than just his own."[17]

Of all of Updike's characters, Harry most convincingly embodies the near-impossibility of remaining true to oneself while also satisfying one's obligations to others in an increasingly amoral world. Like Roth's tortured protagonists, Harry himself is quite aware of the conflicts that beset him. Although he is convinced of the validity of his intuitive longings, he is also attuned—to an extent that no one else in the novel, except perhaps Eccles, is aware—to the ambiguities of his situation, and he does in fact tend to weigh the effects of his actions on others. That he usually rationalizes away the problems ("Ruth and Janice both have parents: with this thought he dissolves both of them") does not alter the fact that, ultimately, "guilt and responsibility slide together . . . inside his chest" (p. 305). When at the end of the novel Harry once again opts to run, he is both culpable and heroic. He has failed to formulate a viable response to life's complexities, yet still refuses to be stifled—or inhibited—by them. Hence his misdeeds occur in a context of both guilt and transcendence.

Tragically, there appears to be no solution, and herein lies another similarity between Roth's and Updike's fiction. Despite their rather different emphases, both seem to imply that the large problems of responsibility and guilt are essentially enigmatic, that there is something in human nature that renders final judgments on such issues impossible. Hence, in both writers' work these questions are left unanswered, creating a sense of irresolution that evokes the perplexing tentativeness of life itself. Despite their desperate efforts toward reconciliation, the characters in Roth's and Updike's fiction seldom reach that goal. At best, they achieve qualified adjustment, and only partial self-understanding. Critic Larry Taylor's remarks concerning Updike's *Of the Farm* are generally applicable to the work of both writers: "The reconciliation and knowledge . . . are by no means a definitive answer to human conflict. The wisdom attained is like the wisdom so often attained by characters in Shakespeare's plays—a matter of melancholy and faltering reconciliation rather than triumphant affirmation, and a matter of subtle concession rather than dramatic capitulation."[18]

5

Secondary Themes in Roth and Updike:
Materialism, Vocation, the Clergy, and Sport

IN ADDITION TO their common interest in the major themes already discussed, Roth and Updike share a preoccupation with several subsidiary concerns as well. Most prominent among these are materialism, the importance—and absence—of truly meaningful work, the "fallen" state of the clergy, and the idea of sport as metaphor. These themes appear throughout the canons of both writers. Occasionally, one or more of these subjects are absolutely fundamental to a given work; elsewhere, and more typically, they function in the service of larger themes. Wherever these secondary issues appear, however, their presence broadens and enriches the writers' explorations of the social landscape.

Yet Roth and Updike tend to handle the subsidiary themes rather differently. The contrasts in their treatment of materialism provide a convenient example: Roth seems more cautionary than hostile toward wealth, while Updike mounts a straightforward attack against money as a source of evil. *Goodbye, Columbus* castigates the world of suburban excess; Roth's opprobrium, however, is not directed at wealth *per se,* but at those who typically amass it. The well-to-do Patimkins and their ilk are depicted as coarse, vulgar *nouveaux riches* whose behavior is inappropriate to their station. As the Paramount film of the novel so comically illustrates, the dinner scene and the wedding scene convey this idea especially well.

Prosperity itself, though, is often presented in Roth's work as a rather positive—if complicated—phenomenon. When Neil observes, for example, that Ben Patimkin "could hardly transmit all the satisfaction and surprise he felt about the life he had managed to build for himself and his family" (p. 105), Roth's approval is plain. And when Neil rhapsodizes about the relative merits of suburbia and Newark, there can be no doubting the advantages of the former. Granted, Neil feels for the city "an attachment so rooted that it could not help but branch out into affection" (p. 41), but his position is akin to that of Eli Peck (in "Eli, the Fanatic") who, even while challenging his neighbors' priorities, notes that the suburbs enjoy unprecedented ease and security.

Neil is quite self-conscious about his origins, and yearns to climb the social ladder. He says that "the hundred and eighty feet that the suburbs rose in altitude above Newark brought one closer to heaven" (p. 18), and the suburbs are continually described in celestial or Edenic terms. At one point, Brenda is even portrayed as an angel of deliverance. Neil toys with the prospect of marrying into Patimkin money, and finds such a notion far from unappealing. What finally drives him away from Brenda is the young woman's personal shortcomings—and those of other family members—rather than any disenchantment with their lifestyle. Where Neil and several of Roth's other protagonists are mistaken is in their naïve supposition that money in itself can solve their problems. Coupled with this belief is the assumption that they are

exempt from the potentially corrupting influences that success might entail.

Almost always in Roth's work, the protagonists seem to regard themselves as somehow intrinsically "worthy" of material privilege, even if those around them are not. The Rothian protagonist has no misgivings about aspiring to material
prosperity and in some cases already qualmlessly enjoys it.
Well-heeled, Harvard-educated Gabe Wallach of *Letting Go*
demonstrates this with his preference for expensive clothing
and his condescension toward those who are materially less
favored than he. After a particularly exorbitant shopping
spree in Brooks Brothers' Chicago store, he extols "the pleasures to be derived from spending money on myself. . . .
There is something life-giving and religious in outfitting
yourself" (p. 168). Neil, who flaunts his single Brooks Brothers shirt, would probably agree. Roth, who has been included on several "Best Dressed Men" lists, might also concur.
But what emerges quite plainly upon a careful reading of
Roth's fictions is that his deeper, underlying message is a
moralistic one: for all its attractions, money alone cannot buy
happiness.

He gives this idea its clearest articulation in *Zuckerman Unbound.* In that book, Nathan Zuckerman becomes an instant
millionaire with his best-selling novel, *Carnovsky.* On one level, his newfound status is a boon, catapulting him into the
heady atmosphere of custom-made suits, chauffeured limou-
sines, investment specialists, and movie actresses, but Zuckerman learns quickly that his wealth and attendant celebrity
are not without their price. "All this, this luck—what did it
mean? Coming so suddenly, and on such a scale, it was as
baffling as a misfortune" (p. 4). Zuckerman's life is changed
overnight, for he can no longer appear in public without risk-

ing harassment. He loses all privacy, as unsolicited attention—well-meaning and otherwise—is lavished upon him.

His fame attracts Alvin Pepler, a former quiz show star
bilked by the producers of "Smart Money" in the 1950s. The
logorrheic "Jewish Marine" is one of the most memorable
secondary characters in recent fiction; reminiscent of Bellow's zany grotesques, he becomes a blend of the spurious
and the genuine. He is quite eccentric—and possibly mad—
yet his desperation and outrage derive from perfectly valid
complaints. Significantly, he is incensed not at having been
cheated out of prize money, but on moral principle. As he
truthfully asserts, "Greed had nothing to do with it. It
was . . . my self-respect. As a man! As a war veteran! As a
war veteran twice over! As a Newarker! As a Jew!" (p. 39). A
would-be writer, Pepler beleaguers Zuckerman for the "secret" to literary success, not because he aspires to material
gain, but because he wants to set the record straight concerning his lost championship and what he envisions as the dam-
age done thereby to the Jewish people. Despite his erratic behavior, and the suggestion that he may be plotting to kidnap
Zuckerman's mother, Pepler serves to remind Zuckerman
that there are more important things than money, and that he
must not permit prosperity to blind him to those more significant considerations: self-respect, honor, loyalty, and integri-
ty. There is much truth to Pepler's eventual charge that Zuckerman is beginning to lose touch with his identity. Largely
because of Pepler's prodding, Zuckerman is roused from his
torpor and forced back into "the vrai"; he returns to Newark—albeit with an armed bodyguard—and comes away
with greater insight into his own circumstances. Through
Pepler's agency, Zuckerman is reminded that money is really
not so crucial, and he is reinforced in his deeper convictions.

Updike proffers a far more emphatically cautionary message: *cupiditas radix malorum est.* In his writings, materialism is

everywhere suspect, as in the opening lines of his early poem "Shillington," where he laments the passing of a bygone and more spartan reality:

> The vacant lots are occupied, the woods
> Diminish, Slate Hill sinks beneath its crown
> Of solvent homes, and marketable goods
> On all sides crowd the good remembered town.[1]

The same ideas—and, in fact, the same general setting—provide the focus for many other passages from Updike's works. In *Of the Farm,* for example, Joey Robinson speaks of the "garish abundance. . . . brightly shoddy goods . . . sordid plenty" (pp. 84–85) of a shopping center near his old hometown. In *Rabbit Is Rich,* Updike speaks ruefully of "shoppers pillaging the malls hacked from the former fields of corn, rye, tomatoes, cabbages, and strawberries" (p. 7). Indeed, in Updike's work the antimaterialistic bias is so pronounced that the poor are actually exalted. This is quite obvious even in his significantly titled first novel, *The Poorhouse Fair,* in which the indigent oldtimers are portrayed as embodying the last vestiges of humanism.

Similarly, in *The Centaur,* much is made of George Caldwell's poverty, which is presented almost as an inverse measure of his saintliness. Unlike Roth's natty protagonists, Caldwell evinces a total disregard for physical appearances. His overcoat, for example, is "a tattered checkered castoff with mismatching buttons, which he had rescued from a church sale, though it was too small and barely reached his knees." His hat is "a hideous blue knitted cap that he had plucked out of a trash barrel. . . . Pulled down over his ears, it made him look like an overgrown dimwit in a comic strip" (p. 64). Fully embracing the conventional Christian outlook, Caldwell ignores worldly matters to ponder more spiritual concerns; he disregards the "treasures of earth" and "lay[s] up . . . treasures in heaven" (Matt. 6:19–20).

Perhaps Updike's most interesting treatment of materialism is in the "Rabbit" novels, where Harry Angstrom's personal stature dwindles as his bankroll grows. In *Rabbit, Run,* Harry shares Caldwell's rejection of the material world, and his pursuit of more intangible forms of self-justification. Although his orientation is essentially secular—he is, for example, a confirmed sensualist—at no point does the young Harry embrace a *materialistic* value system. Indeed, Harry's difficulties stem in large part from his sense of being "ensnared in that . . . trap of material clutter"[2] that serves as a physical extension of the societal obligations and responsibilities that he so resists. Harry often seems actually to be divorced from his belongings, and from the material world. In both *Rabbit, Run* and *Rabbit Redux* he is quite cavalier about financial matters; he is so intent upon his metaphysical quests, dissimilar as they are in the two novels, that he seems almost oblivious to such considerations. He is relatively unmoved, for example, when in *Rabbit Redux* his house is destroyed by arsonists. In a sense, this is an aspect of what could be considered Harry's "redeeming transcendence."

In fact, there is also an actively *anti*materialistic tone that characterizes both books. Wherever wealth appears in the "Rabbit" novels, it invariably serves as an emblem of moral turpitude. Frederick Springer, Harry's father-in-law, exemplifies this. Although rather prosperous, he is guilty of dishonest business practices. In *Rabbit, Run* Harry is reluctantly implicated when Springer gives him a job at the car lot: "The job at the lot is easy enough, if it isn't any work for you to lie. He feels exhausted by midafternoon. You see these clunkers come in with 80,000 miles on them and the pistons so loose the oil just pours through and they get a washing and the

speedometer turned back and you hear yourself saying this
represents a real bargain, owned by a man with two cars and
not 30,000 miles of wear in it. He'll ask forgiveness" (p. 234).
In *Rabbit Redux,* Harry confesses that he despises his affluent
Penn Park neighbors, particularly the physicians. In the
same vein, wealthy Mrs. Aldridge, Jill's mother, is portrayed
in a uniformly negative manner and is at one point termed a
"rich bitch" (p. 348). Surely, Mrs. Aldridge and the Penn
Park doctors have much in common with the wealthy characters portrayed in Updike's "suburban" fictions: *Couples,
Marry Me,* and certain short stories.

But Harry joins their ranks in *Rabbit Is Rich,* and in so doing forfeits his uniqueness. Suddenly he is ensnared in the
material entrapments of upper middle class existence.
Whereas previously he had disdained other people's preoccupation with money, he is now very much caught up in the
same dollar-obsessed scramble. Indeed, his wife Janice tells
him, "Money. . . . That's all you ever think about" (p. 44),
while his son Nelson asks, "Dad, how can you keep thinking
about money all the time?" (p. 345). Although Harry is now
somewhat more self-assured, and therefore more accepting
of life's disappointments and frustrations, Updike clearly intends that we should see Harry as badly diminished. Certainly the novel's title is thoroughly ironic. At one point, Updike
likens the activities of a currency exchange to "peddling
smut" (p. 210), and when Harry and Janice are shown struggling along a downtown Brewer street with their $14,662.50
in silver dollars, Updike's description is absolutely contemp-
tuous:

He keeps having to wait for Janice to catch up, while his own burden, double hers, pulls at his arms. . . . He is sweating across his
back beneath his expensive overcoat and his shirt collar keeps dry-

ing to a clammy cold edge. During these waits he stares up Weiser toward the mauve and brown bulk of Mt. Judge; in his eyes as a child God had reposed on the slopes of that mountain, and now he can imagine how through God's eyes from that vantage he and Janice might look below: two ants trying to make it up the sides of a bathroom basin. (p. 371)

Finally, Harry "glimpses the truth that to be rich is to be robbed, to be rich is to be poor" (p. 375).

In *Rabbit Is Rich* and the other "Rabbit" novels, the enduring impression is that Updike views material prosperity almost as a guarantee of moral dissolution. The suggestion is that Updike's suburbanites are, in a sense, freed by their wealth from moral responsibility—at least in their own eyes. Their constant posturing, partying, and profligacy is presented as a condition of their station. Updike has commented on this at some length:

I think what's happened to the American middle class is that it is trying to prove that they have open to it almost the whole range of freedom that had hitherto been enjoyed solely by the aristocracies of Europe and Asia. But the capacities of past and present societies to bear, psychologically, the consequences of this freedom are rather different. The aristocrats were never very numerous . . . . But in America today, you have millions of people trying to live aristocratically. Inevitably this produces disjunctions.[3]

Not the least of the "disjunctions" is contemporary America's cynically indifferent or even hostile outlook with regard to vocation and work. Although in Updike's oeuvre this phenomenon is directly related to the broader issue of pernicious materialism, in the fiction of both Roth and Updike it is also a separate topic in its own right, one that both writers return to again and again in their explorations of American life. Repeatedly, these writers' characters reveal singularly alienated attitudes toward their jobs. Of course, this aspect of Roth's and Updike's fiction can be considered just another example of their realism—such feelings are, after all, distressingly commonplace in actuality—but it goes deeper than simply that; it becomes a highly noticeable and characteristic feature of both writers' work. Unable to achieve personal satisfaction, Roth's and Updike's questing protagonists feel dislocated in every area of their lives; hence, their jobs fail to provide a sense of purpose or accomplishment, but instead seem empty and devoid of meaning.

Among Roth's protagonists are a librarian (Neil Klugman), a high ranking bureaucrat (Portnoy), a whole gallery of professor-writers (Gabe Wallach, Peter Tarnopol, David Kepesh, and Nathan Zuckerman), and—if we include the collected short fiction—an army officer (Nathan Marx), a businessman (Lou Epstein), and an attorney (Eli Peck). But despite their various levels of professional status and the fact that practically all of these characters are at least reasonably successful at their jobs, most of Roth's protagonists seem to derive only moderate satisfaction from their work. They go through the motions, doing what is required and expected of them; usually, though, there is scant conviction in their actions, and little real dedication. Inevitably, even in those instances where a character is *initially* enthusiastic about his calling, the individual's work becomes either enervating or burdensome, or irrelevant to his most deeply felt needs. Neil, for example, ridicules his career-oriented coworkers and asserts that the "library was not going to be my life-work, I knew it. . . . I never quite knew how I'd gotten there or why I stayed" (pp. 42–43). Similarly, Eli Peck finds that his profession is frustrating: "being a lawyer surrounded him like quicksand. . . . the law didn't seem to be the answer . . . . And that, of course, made him feel foolish and unnecessary" (p. 268).

In a less negative but decidedly unenthusiastic vein, Gabe Wallach confides that his career is of secondary importance to him. He admits that he teaches "out of neither spiritual nor financial urgency," and that "in the end I knew it was not from my students or my colleagues . . . but from my private life, my secret life, that I would extract whatever joy—or whatever misery—was going to be mine" (pp. 229–30). The bitingly sarcastic view of academe that emerges from Gabe's account of life as a University of Chicago faculty member has been frequently cited as a masterpiece of "academic satire." Yet Gabe's comments are unwittingly ironic, for his personal life is not only disappointing in itself, but eventually sours his professional life as well.

This is equally true of Roth's authors. In *My Life as a Man*, Tarnopol, whose early enthusiasm for writing and teaching is seemingly unbounded, ultimately becomes "blocked" (like Updike's Henry Bech), and confesses that his "writing . . . was wholly at the mercy of . . . marital confusion" (p. 104) and that he has become "hopeless at my work . . . [because] miserable in . . . marriage" (p. 105). Roth's most successful novelist, Nathan Zuckerman, achieves best sellerdom and subsequent fame. But in *The Anatomy Lesson* he decides "to escape his art, to be released from . . . the readers and from the meaning given to his work, from the relentless self-consciousness and the endless self-mining and the moral paradoxes inherent in the vocation, and, at the age of 40, to go to medical school and become a doctor instead."[4] Roth's view would seem to be that for a healthy, productive professional life to obtain, the individual must be fully at peace otherwise. Since none of his protagonists are so reconciled with themselves, their careers become hellish reflections of their disordered personal lives.

This applies even to Alexander Portnoy, one of the most prominent and accomplished of Roth's professionals. Although he is "Assistant Commissioner for the City of New York Commission on Human Opportunity," and prides himself on his achievements, he is also acutely aware of the discrepancies between his private and public selves. His real, inner self cannot be fulfilled, except by a rejection and repudiation of the very respectability that his position entails. Accordingly, he repeatedly accuses himself of insincerity and phoniness, as in the following (imagined) exchange:

"Please, don't you read the *New York Times*? I have spent my whole adult life protecting the rights of the defenseless! Five years I was with the ACLU, fighting the good fight for practically nothing. And before that a Congressional committee! I could make twice, *three* times the money in a practice of my own, but I don't! I don't! Now I have been appointed—don't you read the papers!—I am now Assistant Commissioner of Human Opportunity! Preparing a special report on bias in the building trades—"Bull*shit*. Commissioner of Cunt, that's who you are! Commissioner of Human Opportunists! Oh, you jerk-off artist! You case of arrested development! All is vanity, Portnoy, but you really take the cake! A hundred and fifty-eight points of I.Q. and all of it right down the drain! A lot of good it did to skip those two grades of grammar school, you dummy!" (p. 204).

Aware of his schizophrenic weakness and the resulting hypocrisy that it engenders, Portnoy is left in a state of ambivalence toward his job. Although by day he is an able and respected public official, privately he is a slavering hedonist rather like David Kepesh of *The Professor of Desire*. This conflict gives rise in his imagination to fantasies of public revelations of his true nature, as in the comical headlines that he envisions: "ASST HUMAN OPP'Y COMMISH FOUND HEADLESS IN GO-GO GIRL'S APT!" (p. 161) and "ASST HUMAN OPP'Y COMMISH FLOGS DUMMY, *Also Lives in Sin, Reports Old School Chum*" (p. 175). In short, Portnoy is stymied, caught in a love-hate relationship with his job, and of course this dilemma serves as an effective metaphor for his larger predicament.

As with so many of the points discussed in this study, the basic difference between Roth's and Updike's handling of the question of vocation is that while Roth typically adopts a character-centered, individualized, psychological approach to the issue, Updike employs a broader, more sociologically oriented perspective. In Roth, the protagonists' dilemmas must finally be seen as resulting from their own emotional and psychological confusions, while Updike's thesis is that individuals experience difficulty largely because of being caught up in the overpowering currents of swift cultural change. Updike repeatedly asserts that much of what passes for "work" in the modern world is really a bogus imitation, a charade. He implies, though, that this is not the fault of the characters involved; rather, it is presented as evidence of a generalized cultural and moral shoddiness, a collective "fall from grace." He returns frequently to the ideas of a lost but somehow more viable American past in which one's work was truly integral to the person's life, and in large part defined the individual's purpose: "My novels are all about the search for useful work . . . . So many people these days have to sell things they don't believe in, and have jobs that defy describing. It's so different from the time when men even took their names from the work they did—Carpenter, Farmer, Fisher. A man has to build his life outward from a job he can do."[5]

In Updike's fiction, work takes on an almost religious dimension that reflects the author's grounding in traditional Protestant theology. A phrase such as "the Protestant work ethic" is perhaps too reductive; nevertheless, the Christian conception of work as a form of prayer permeates Updike's fiction. And the suggestion plainly is that America's present spiritual laxity is reflected in current attitudes toward employment. Whereas people once found purpose and direction in their work, many now view their professional obligations as barriers and impediments. The spiritual component has been negated, producing a culture in which people labor without fulfillment. In *Bech: A Book,* the title character is a writer who can no longer write. And at the outset of *Bech Is Back,* wherein he does finally complete another novel, Bech "could not even write his own name."[6] Joey Robinson in *Of the Farm* speaks of actual physical labor as providing "proof, as my real work never gives me, of work done" (p. 64). His mother complains that there are "so few jobs that seem to *do* anything" (p. 110). In *A Month of Sundays,* the Reverend Mr. Marshfield speaks of "our impossible and often mischievously idle jobs."[7] The world of *Couples* is "a place where foolish work must be done to support fleeting pleasures" (pp. 138–39) and the characters do not really work but "perform . . . impersonations of working men, of stockbrokers and dentists and engineers" (p. 74).

Updike believes that contemporary work is somehow a pale distortion, a counterfeit, of what once was. Repeatedly, therefore, those who practice crafts are exalted, as Updike's other characters voice doleful admiration for this vanishing breed, who are conspicuous precisely because they are anomalous. Such are the "venerable carpenters, Adams and Comeau" (p. 84) of *Couples,* holdovers from an era "before bastard materials and bastard crafts eclipsed honest carpentry, and work was replaced by delays and finagling" (p. 195). Similarly, in *Rabbit Redux,* old Kurt Schrack, the foreign language typesetter, is described as "likable in that he had done something scrupulously that others could not do at all" (p. 28). Certainly this idea is absolutely central to short stories like "Plumbing" (in *Museums and Women*) and "The Gun Shop" (in *Problems*), both of which suggest that the skilled artisan's craft is among our most enduring stays against mutability and flux—and hence against mortality.

Not incidentally, each of Updike's most "heroic" characters—John Hook, Rabbit, George Caldwell, Piet Hanema— possesses some skill, ability, or area of expertise that elevates him above his peers and qualifies him as a "craftsman," in effect if not in fact. Hook and Caldwell, for example, are teachers. Piet, irrespective of his other shortcomings, is exceptional among the men of *Couples* in being a dedicated carpenter, committed to excellence in his field.

The young Harry Angstrom, of course, excels in sports, which for him becomes a sort of calling. That is part of his problem; his "craft" is unmarketable, and he spends the rest of his life engaged in unstimulating employment. In *Rabbit, Run* he demonstrates the Magipeel kitchen gadget in dime stores, and later is relegated to "cheating people in used-car lots" (p. 270) for his father-in-law. In *Rabbit Redux,* he learns a more worthy skill—typesetting—but is fired because of encroaching automation (another instance of Updike's indictment of contemporary priorities). And in *Rabbit Is Rich,* an almost totally compromised Harry has now inherited the Springer car dealership and actually runs the business he earlier scorned. Moreover, he knows that even this inglorious occupation has lost whatever challenges it may once have held. As chief salesman Charlie Stavros puts it, "This isn't selling. It's like supermarkets now: it's shelf-stacking, and ringing it out at the register. When it was all used, we used to try to fit a car to every customer. Now it's take it or leave it. With this seller's market there's no room to improvise" (p. 223). Harry has achieved a degree of material stability and has convinced himself that his life is satisfactory, but really he has allowed the spark of his individuality to be extinguished. His present, diminished self is in sharp contrast to his former identity, and the disparity is heightened by the yellowing newspaper clippings on the dealership wall, accounts of Harry's long-ago exploits on the basketball court. Only Harry's restlessness remains, an inner hunger that manifests itself in impetuous, misdirected gestures (such as his attempts to locate his daughter by Ruth Leonard) and occasional—largely disappointing—sexual forays. Like so many other characters in Updike's fiction, the Harry Angstrom of *Rabbit Is Rich* labors for material gain alone, at the expense of his metaphysical well-being. Certainly the problem of vocation is central for Updike, as it is for Roth.

Among the most disturbing features of these writers' treatment of occupational malaise is their mutual suggestion that the modern clergy—who should ideally serve as a source of strength and good counsel—have fared no better than anyone else in the performance of their "professional duties," and, in view of their vitally crucial role, can be considered to have failed even more drastically. A veritable rogues' gallery of pompous, inept, and hypocritical clergymen populates Roth's and Updike's fiction, serving as yet another index of these authors' shared belief that on all fronts American society is suffering a steady, inexorable erosion.

Of course, Roth's wise old Rabbi Tzuref in "Eli, the Fanatic" is an obvious exception, serving as the moral center of that story. But Tzuref, a D.P., is clearly intended as an "Old World" figure, anomalous in modern America. Indeed, this very discrepancy is at the heart of the story as Tzuref's traditional values are juxtaposed against those of present-day suburban Jewry. Usually, however, Roth's rabbis are an unattractive lot. As with so many aspects of Roth's fiction, *Portnoy's Complaint* provides the best example. In Rabbi Warshaw ("Fat Warshaw, the Reb. My stout and pompous spiritual leader!" [p. 201]), Roth creates a figure intended to evoke not only laughter but scorn, as the young Portnoy demythologizes not only the individual rabbi, but the rabbinate at large:

Mother, Rabbi Warshaw is a fat, pompous impatient fraud, with an absolutely grotesque superiority complex, a character out of Dickens is what he is, someone who if you stood next to him on the bus and didn't know he was so revered, you would say, "That man stinks to high heaven of cigarettes," and that is *all* you would say. . . . if you want to feel pious about somebody, feel pious about my father, God damn it, and bow down to him the way you bow down to that big fat comical son of a bitch, because my father *really* works his balls off and doesn't happen to think that he is God's special assistant into the bargain . . . . Oh God, oh Guh-ah-duh, if you're up there shining down your countenance, why not spare us from here on out the enunciation of the rabbis! Why not spare us the rabbis themselves! Look, why not spare us religion, if only in the name of our human dignity! (pp. 73–74)

Roth's skepticism toward the rabbinate provides the basis for the *Goodbye, Columbus* short story "The Conversion of the Jews," in which young Ozzie Freedman's habit of demanding answers to difficult questions has placed him in an adversary relationship with his religion instructor, Rabbi Binder. Surely Roth's choice of names here is deliberate. Ozzie wishes to make full use of the so-called "free discussion" periods; the rabbi, young but doctrinaire, restricts the students to traditionalistic interpretations of theological matters. Ozzie bri-

dles at such teachings as the concept of the "chosen people,"
his mother's habit of viewing life from an exclusively Jewish
perspective, and (at the moment the story opens) Binder's re-
fusal to grant the possibility that God could permit a virgin
birth—specifically, the birth of Christ. Logically, Ozzie reasons that if God could call into being all of creation, then
surely the arranging of a virgin birth would be within his
powers:

I asked the question about God, how if he could create the heaven
and earth in six days, and make all the animals and the fish and the
light in six days—the light especially, that's what always gets me,
that He could make the light. Making fish and animals, that's pret-
ty good—. . . . But making light . . . I mean when you think
about it, it's really something. . . . Anyway, I asked Binder if He
could make all that in six days, and He could *pick* the six days He
wanted right out of nowhere, why couldn't he let a woman have a
baby without having intercourse. (pp. 152–53)

But Binder equivocates on this, and Ozzie feels that "he
was trying to make me look stupid" (p. 154). Ozzie's resentment grows, as does Binder's belief that the boy is "deliberately . . . a wise guy" (p. 154). When the virgin birth issue
again becomes a point of contention, Ozzie brashly asserts,
"You don't know! You don't know anything about God!"
(p. 158). At this point the story veers toward hyperbole:
Binder strikes Ozzie, who flees to the synagogue roof; after
some confusion, Ozzie forces the crowd gathered below—his
mother, his classmates, the caretaker, Binder, and a contingent of net-wielding firemen—to kneel in the Christian position of prayer and "first one at a time, then all together"
(p. 170) acknowledge aloud that God is omnipotent, that he
could "make a child without intercourse" (p. 170), that they
believe in the divinity of Christ, and that religious beliefs

should not be imposed by force; symbolically, Ozzie then leaps "right into the center of the . . . net that glowed . . . like an overgrown halo" (p. 171).

Although the story's concluding scene is implausible enough to have prompted at least one critic to interpret the rooftop episode simply as Ozzie's "wish fulfilling dream . . . fantasized,"[8] there is no evidence for other than a literal reading. "The Conversion of the Jews" conveys an emphatic message, as it juxtaposes two very different conceptions of religious belief. Certain factors, however, should be kept in mind. Ozzie's position is neither profound nor radical. He seeks not really to challenge the traditional belief, but to see it validated. And this validation is, of course, what Binder is unable to provide. It is in this respect—the concept of clerical inadequacy—that the story is most closely related to Updike's treatment of the Protestant ministry.

Updike has been—if slightly less vituperative than Roth— no less critical in this area. In fact, he has used clerical characters considerably more often than Roth has, introducing them into many of his novels and stories. Even in his first novel, *The Poorhouse Fair,* there is a reference to "the strained, or bluff, expressions on the faces of the . . . clergy" (p. 106), and this skeptically wary tone has continued to characterize Updike's depictions of ministers. There is the supercilious Reverend Mr. March of *The Centaur,* for example. Engrossed in flirtatious badinage with a female gym teacher, he snubs George Caldwell's plea for spiritual guidance. "Come to my study any morning but Wednesdays," March dismissively tells him, "I'll lend you some excellent books" (p. 253). Similarly, the young minister in *Of the Farm* is described as having a pale face, "a nasal pedantic voice. . . . [a] limp and chill little hand" (pp. 149, 154). He preaches a polished but hypocritically sanctimonious sermon on the relationship between the sexes; it is rumored that "his eyes rove. . . . There's been talk," and Mrs. Robinson sagely avers that "whenever a man begins to talk that way, he's trying to excuse himself from some woman's pain" (p. 154). The fatuous Reverend Mr. Pedrick of *Couples* is termed "a skeletal ignorant man" having "delusions . . . about money," who "sought to transpose the dessicated forms of Christianity into financial terms" (pp. 20, 21). The Reverend Mr. Eccles and the Reverend Mr. Kruppenbach in *Rabbit, Run* embody—in opposite but equally mistaken ways—the general failure of institutionalized religion, while the Reverend Mr. Campbell in *Rabbit Is Rich* is presented as a shallow pretender.

Given Updike's abiding interest in religion—he is considered something of a lay expert on the subject, and has published numerous reviews and essays on theological topics—it is consistent that in *A Month of Sundays* he chose to employ a minister centrally, as protagonist. Although the Reverend Thomas Marshfield is rather sympathetically (and humorously) drawn, the book is fully consonant with Updike's accustomed mode of censorious qualification when depicting men of the cloth, while at the same time it also provides a forthright fictional elaboration of the author's theological perspective.

Revealed as a redoubtable adulterer, a "doubting Thomas" whose sermons seem always to become paeans to the *deus absconditus*, the Reverend Mr. Marshfield has been banished to a desert sanitarium for wayward clergy. Despite the book's "cute" aspects—one of the women seduced by Marshfield is the church organist (such puns abound); Marshfield's wife's maiden name is Chillingworth, and she is the daughter of his former ethics teacher; the retreat house is run by Ms. Prynne; and the name of one of the other errant ministers, Amos, is an acronym for the novel's title—it is thematically in line with Updike's other fiction. Marshfield's dilemma is essentially the same as that which besets many another Updike protagonist—most notably, Rabbit, Piet Hanema, and Jerry Conant. He is torn between spirituality and sensuality, a dichotomy symbolized by his two sons, "a Spartan and a Sybarite" (p. 123).

Marshfield attempts to reconcile these opposed impulses through a prescribed regimen of golfing, card playing, and, most importantly, free writing. The thirty-one ensuing daily journal entries—including four highly significant sermons that correspond to his four Sundays in exile—constitute a sort of mock-Augustinian confession and the written record of Marshfield's spiritual quest. On the one hand, he celebrates the hedonistic, even asserting that in our sensuality we find our fullest human expression and hence our most intense spirituality. In this, Marshfield's musings are similar to Neil Klugman's internal monologue in Roth's *Goodbye, Columbus:* "If we meet You at all, God, it's that we're carnal . . . and thereby partake of You. I am carnal, and I know You approve, I just know it" (p. 111). Specifically, Marshfield exalts adultery, elevating it to the status of a sacrament:

Adultery, my friends, is our inherent condition. . . . who that has eyes to see cannot so lust? . . . Adultery is not a choice to be avoided; it is a circumstance to be embraced. . . . Wherein does the modern American man recover his sense of worth, not as dogged breadwinner and economic integer, but as romantic minister and phallic knight, as personage, embodiment, and hero? In adultery. And wherein does the American woman, coded into mindlessness by household slavery and the stupefying companionship of greedy infants, recover her powers of decision, of daring, of discrimination. . . ? In adultery. . . . They meet in love, for love, with love; they tremble in a glory that is unpolluted by the wisdom of this world; they are, truly, children of light. . . . Verily, the sacrament of marriage, as instituted in its adamant impossibility by our Sav-

ior, exists but as a precondition for the sacrament of adultery.
. . . We *are* an adulterous generation; let us rejoice. (pp. 44–47)

At the same time, however, Marshfield rejects the liberal,
works-oriented theological outlook embraced by his father
(also a minister) and holds firmly to a traditional belief in
Christ as God incarnate. Like Updike, Marshfield is Barth-
ian in his religious philosophy, espousing a basic conservatism that is obvious in passages such as this one, in which
Marshfield ridicules his curate, accusing him of various delusions: "limp-wristed theology, a perfectly custardly confec-
tion of Jungian-Reichian soma-mysticism swimming in a
soupy caramel of Tillichic, Jasperian, Bultmannish blather,
all served up in a dime-store dish of his gutless generation's
give-away Gemütlichkeit" (p. 13). In quoting St. Paul—
"We are of all men most miserable. . . . if Christ be not ris-
en" (p. 205)—Marshfield echoes Updike himself, who in
"Seven Stanzas at Easter" affirms a strictly literal interpreta-
tion of the Resurrection:

> Make no mistake: if He rose at all
> It was as His body;
> if the cells' dissolution did not reverse, the
>   molecules reknit, the amino acids rekindle,
> the Church will fall.[9]

Concomitantly, though, Marshfield agonizes over the irrational brutality of the physical universe, cataloguing its hor-
rors: "the pain of infants, the inexorability of disease, the
wantonness of fortune, the billions of fossilized deaths, the
helplessness of the young, the idiocy of the old, the crafts-
manship of torturers, the authority of blunderers, the savage-
ry of accident, the unbreatheability of water, and all the other
repulsive flecks on the face of Creation" (p. 38). Surely, the

remembered rest home scenes involving Marshfield's senile father, despite their obvious comic elements, are an example of Marshfield's grimly unblinking response to the more harrowing possibilities of existence. But despite the book's many images of death and termination—Marshfield's retreat house, for example, is omega-shaped—Marshfield refuses to despair. Increasingly his sermons focus on life, and he seems to experience a rebirth of faith.

Nevertheless, the form that Marshfield's spiritual resurgence takes remains rather problematic. His eventual copulation (whether real or imagined, or with Ms. Prynne or the reader, or a combination of both—this is not clear) would indicate that Marshfield's spiritual journey has come full circle. There is no indication that he is about to mend his ways. If anything, the opposite is presaged. He has not learned to moderate his earthly desires, but has learned to simply accept as natural and fitting the conflict between them and his supposed duties as a cleric. One imagines, however, that this resolution, not unlike Harry's in *Rabbit, Run,* bodes ill for Marshfield's continued employment as a minister, given society's traditionally restrictive notions of what constitutes proper behavior for the clergy. This may well be the point. Updike seems to suggest in all his works that conventional conceptions of propriety and morality are too simplistically rule oriented, too concerned with surface issues, too unmindful of the more transcendently spiritual aspects of life. Wherever clergymen appear in his work, this is immediately evident. Either they struggle with the conflict between their own and society's values (like Marshfield and Eccles), or they fail in their ministry by becoming either too rigidly conventional (like Kruppenbach), or worse, too pragmatically secular (like March, Pedrick, or Campbell). Updike seems to be suggesting, just as Roth does, that the modern clergyman has adopted a position unfaithful to both the spirit and the letter of the moral law. Roth and Updike imply that the clergy's various forms of indecisive accommodation to the dislocations of our times are among the clearest and most unsettling indices of those communal confusions. As Benjamin DeMott explains, "Everywhere on the contemporary scene the faithless lead the faithless; the quality of this general experience for leaders and followers alike—the breathless hypocrisy of it, the ceaseless veerings toward, then away from, truth—has an edge of significance; probing clerical insides is a way of showing forth the significance."[10]

In view of all these difficulties, it is hardly surprising that many of Roth's and Updike's characters yearn to escape the strains and confusions of the present, and frequently entertain wry, wistfully nostalgic reminiscences of their childhood and youth, a time when American realities—or, perhaps more accurately, the characters' conceptions of them—were somehow less complex, more orderly and logical in their moral outlines. Often, the fantasy of a return to innocence revolves around an idealized conception of athletics, and this is one of the several ways that Roth and Updike employ the idea of sport as metaphor, another of the recurring secondary themes that serve to link these writers' fictions. Indeed, an entire doctoral dissertation has been written on the subject.[11]

In the autobiographical essay "My Baseball Years," Roth reveals his affection for the game:

this game that I loved with all my heart not simply for the fun of playing it (fun was secondary, really), but for the mythic and esthetic dimension that it gave to an American boy's life (particularly one whose grandparents hardly spoke English). For someone whose roots in America were strong but only inches deep, and who had no experience, such as a Catholic child might, of an awesome hierarchy that was real and felt, baseball was a kind of secular church that reached into every class and region of the nation and bound us to-gether in common concerns, loyalties, rituals, enthusiasms, and antagonisms.[12]

Similarly, Alexander Portnoy's recollections of childhood ballgames evoke a halcyon world of sharply defined rules and boundaries that conveniently dictate the rights and wrongs, the good and evil, of one's existence. Like Roth, Portnoy conjures up the mythical quality of the experience, invoking legendary names—Joe DiMaggio, Duke Snider, Eddie Wait-kus, Al Gionfriddo—and events, but he also focuses quite in-tensely on the actual playing of the game:

Thank God for center field! Doctor, you can't imagine how truly glorious it is out there, so alone in all that space. . . . center field is like some observation post, a kind of control tower, where you are able to see everything and everyone, to understand what's happen-ing the instant it happens. . . . "It's mine," you call, "it's mine," and then after it you go. For in center field, if you can get to it, it *is* yours. . . . there are people who feel in life the ease, the self-assur-ance, the simple and essential affiliation with what is going on, that I used to feel as a center fielder. . . . one knew exactly, and down to the smallest particular, how a center fielder should conduct himself. . . . Oh, to be a center fielder, a center fielder—and nothing more! (pp. 69, 72)

Updike's Harry Angstrom is another example of the ex-ath-lete who longs to recapture the sense of purpose and direction that he once enjoyed. A former scoring champion, Harry ruefully tells the Reverend Mr. Eccles, "I once played a game real well. I really did. And after you're first-rate at some-thing, no matter what, it kind of takes the kick out of being second-rate" (p. 105). Like Portnoy, Harry yearns to be back in high school, to recapture the sense of ultimate authority and harmony, and the kinesthetic fusion of mind and body that sport afforded him.

Occasionally, Roth's and Updike's characters will reinvolve themselves in athletics in an attempt to redefine the present. The results vary. Sometimes, as with Marshfield's golfing in *A Month of Sundays,* the listless tennis games between father and son in *Letting Go,* or Harry's jogging in *Rabbit Is Rich,* the activity proves futile. Elsewhere, however, as with Harry's pick-up basketball game in the opening scene of *Rabbit, Run,* or his golfing in that novel, adulthood athletic endeavors yield high dividends. Harry's domination of the boys in the scrimmage revitalizes him, for example, and his (often analyzed) perfect tee shot while golfing with Eccles is surely a symbol of the transcendent "otherness" that motivates him:

he looks at the ball, which . . . already seems free of the ground. Very simply he brings the clubhead around his shoulder into it. The sound has a hollowness, a singleness he hasn't heard before. His arms force his head up and his ball is hung way out, lunarly pale against the beautiful black blue of storm clouds. . . . It recedes along a line straight as a ruler-edge. Stricken; sphere, star, speck. It hesitates, and Rabbit thinks it will die, but he's fooled, for the ball makes this hesitation the ground of a final leap: with a kind of visible sob takes a last bite of space before vanishing in falling. "That's *it!*" he cries and, turning to Eccles with a smile of aggrandizement, repeats, "That's it." (pp. 133–34)

Elsewhere Roth and Updike use sport metaphorically in other contexts. Both, for example, have employed it negatively, suggesting that there is something rather puerile about the American preoccupation with games—and, by extension, about the society at large. Roth does this most obviously in *Our Gang,* in which President Trick E. Dixon wears a football uniform while confering with his advisors. In *Rabbit Redux,* Harry, his son, and his father-in-law attend a minor-league baseball game, but again, sport functions negatively, as the scene depicted is disappointing. The implication is that something vital has gone out of the national pastime, and out of the nation itself:

Something has gone wrong. The ball game is boring. The spaced dance of the men in white fails to enchant, the code beneath the staccato spurts of distant motion refuses to yield its meaning. Though basketball was his sport, Rabbit remembers . . . a beauty here bigger than the hurtling beauty of basketball, a beauty refined from country pastures, a game of solitariness. . . . a game whose very taste . . . was America. . . . Rabbit waits for this beauty to rise to him . . . but something is wrong. The crowd is sparse. . . . Sparse, loud, hard: only the drunks, the bookies, the cripples, the senile, and the delinquents come out to the ball park on a Saturday afternoon. Their catcalls are coarse and unkind. . . . And . . . the players themselves . . . seem expert listlessly. . . . they seem specialists like any other, not men playing a game because all men are boys time is trying to outsmart. (pp. 83–84)

In Updike's suburban fictions, sport is presented as simply another context for moral corruption, as tennis, volleyball, and the like become simply a part of the endless round of pointless activities that the adulterers embrace in their attempt to blunt reality. This is especially noticeable in *Rabbit Is Rich,* as Harry's sluggish attempts at jogging, tennis, and golf contrast sharply with his earlier, wholehearted involvement in sport.

So much has been written about the role of basketball in the "Rabbit" novels that to address the topic at length here would be redundant, yet certain features of the subject are worthy of mention. Aside from providing several memorable images, such as Harry's adolescent conception that "the sky of a Saturday morning was the blank scoreboard of a long game about to begin"(p. 39), the game serves well its purpose of shedding light on Harry's inner workings. With one clearly visible goal suspended above the heads of the players, basketball is certainly an apt metaphor for Harry's "upper-directedness." Not surprisingly, he detests the game of golf, with its circuitous route, its multiple goals (often hidden or obstructed, and surrounded by traps and snares) and its downward orientation. It is quite relevant that Harry experiences his one moment of transcendent glory on the links (the perfect tee shot) while driving, rather than putting, and pays no heed to where the ball eventually lands. It is in the ball's upward trajectory that Harry exults.

But the metaphors in *Rabbit, Run* are far from simple. As Joyce Markle has correctly noted, the basketball imagery is part of an intricate pattern: "the basic image in *Rabbit, Run* combines basketball, sex, and religion into a solid geometry of ups and downs, circles and straight lines, nets and spaces."[13] Moreover, if sport functions as an index of Harry's positive qualities, it also serves to reveal the less savory side of his personality, as well. Harry's style of play—heedless, self-centered, headlong—is consistent with his mode of living. In his exaggerated but futile efforts to avoid entanglement and break through to a solitary realm of independent fulfillment, he exercises the selfsame tendencies that marked his performances in basketball. Although he was once a bona fide star capable of scoring thirty-seven points in a single game, his ex-teammate Ronnie Harrison claims that "the whole school knew" that Harry was "not a team player" (p. 177–78), an allegation supposedly voiced first by their coach. We are reminded of Harry's ironically self-deluded remarks concerning his fans: "the crowd . . . seemed right inside you. . . . There was one fat guy used to come who'd get on the floor of Rabbit's stomach and really make it shake. 'Hey, Gunner! Hey, Showboat, shoot! Shoot!' Rabbit remembers him fondly now; to that guy he had been a hero of sorts" (p. 37).

As I have argued elsewhere, the fat man's choice of words, and Harry's apparent sublimation of their true meaning, are quite significant.[14] Clearly, Harry was not a "hero" to this fan, for the appellations "Gunner" and "Showboat" reflect an attitude of jeering disapproval. The latter word, when used as a verb, means to "show off," and has been used in that context at least since 1951, the time of the events in question.[15] In fact, Harry himself uses the term in its properly belittling sense during a conversation with Harrison (p. 177). Similarly, "gunner" is also a term of opprobrium, a derogatory epithet applied to a selfish player who monopolizes the ball, shooting it indiscriminately rather than passing it to a more advantageously positioned teammate.[16] Regardless of the truth or falsity of these accusations—there is some evidence that they are warranted—the point is that Harry represses the actual meaning of the fat man's cries, thereby failing to recognize the extent to which his self-centered play taints his success. Just as surely as basketball requires team play, a legitimately adult response to life presupposes the acceptance of interpersonal responsibility. In playing basketball "not as the crowd thought for the sake of the score but for yourself, in a kind of idleness" (p. 37), Harry prefigures his later lack of commitment.

If *Rabbit, Run* is Updike's most fully developed venture in the use of sport as metaphor, *Goodbye, Columbus* figures rather prominently in Roth's canon in this regard, as Roth uses sports metaphorically to convey character, to reinforce the fact of the Patimkins' wealth and material privilege, and to support the sense of separation between the social classes. Far and away the most elaborate example of the use of sport as metaphor in the work of either writer, however, is Roth's long, experimental *Great American Novel*. Ostensibly the story of the Ruppert Mundys, a fictitious World War II-era baseball team in the mythical Patriot League, the book chronicles the bizarre misadventures of this grotesque contingent of variously disabled and outlandishly named would-be ballplayers. Their collective and individual misfortunes reach nearly epic proportions: they suffer 120 losses in a single season, are dispossessed of their home stadium, and are eventually expunged from the annals of organized sport. The Mundys' madcap saga can be read in several ways. Like "On the Air," *The Great American Novel* is a direct attempt on Roth's part to respond to the untenable American reality that he so strenuously decried in his "Writing American Fiction" essay: "the collapse of the Mundys, a team of incompetent but basically honest and genuine ballplayers, is meant to mirror the replacement of an authentic American popular culture by one that is spurious and dishonest and wholly mercenary."[17] Accordingly, even "The Great American Novel" itself becomes a target of Roth's satiric onslaught, as such giants as Poe, Hawthorne, Melville, and Hemingway (who actually appears as a character—or caricature—in the novel) are invoked, only to be relegated to the level of burlesque farce that constitutes the book's prevailing mode.

Although Roth once again channels the action through a first-person narrator, in this case a cantankerous, eighty-seven-year-old sportswriter named Word Smith,[18] and although he again chooses Newark, New Jersey as the setting for his fiction, *The Great American Novel* bears very little resemblance to his earlier works. In the first place, "Smitty" (unlike, say, Neil Klugman or Alexander Portnoy) functions not as a significant presence in the book, but simply as a literary device, a convenient means whereby the novel's larger thematic concerns are revealed to the reader. Indeed, characterization in *The Great American Novel* is in every instance subordinate to theme. In this respect especially, *The Great American Novel* represented a real departure for Roth in that it attempts to achieve its ends not so much by narrating any one individual's misadventures for their own sake (although Smitty's personal vendetta against the powers-that-be provides a nominal context), but by adopting a broadly panoramic approach, a nearly Pynchonesque dispersion that enables Roth to debunk on several levels simultaneously. Despite the novel's manic texture, Roth is seeking to make in *The Great American Novel* a rather large, comprehensive, and ultimately serious statement. He has explained his use of the seemingly trivial, baseball-centered setting:

It was . . . a matter of . . . discovering in baseball a means to dramatize the *struggle* between the benign national myth of itself that a great power prefers to perpetuate, and the relentlessly insidious, very nearly demonic reality. . . . to admit to the discovery of thematic reverberations, of depth, of overtone, finally of meaning, would seem to contradict what I have said about wanting fundamentally to be unserious; and it does. Yet out of this opposition, or rather out of the attempt to maintain these contradictory impulses in a state of contentious equilibrium, the book evolved. . . . his [Smitty's] are not so unlike the sort of fantasies with which the national imagination began to be plagued during this last demythologizing decade of disorder, upheaval, assassination, and war. . . . Smitty is to my mind correct in aligning himself with Melville and Hawthorne, whom he calls "my precursors, my kinsmen." They too were in search of some encapsulating fiction, or legend, that would, in its own oblique, charged, and cryptic way, constitute the "truth" about the national disease.[19]

For Roth, baseball serves as that "myth" or "legend," as he succeeds in exposing not only the "truth" about the Mundys, but something much broader, which Ben Siegel terms "the disparity in American life between appearance and reality, between professed idealism or good will and an underlying self-seeking grossness or vulgarity."[20]

Since Roth and Updike are, in a sense, social historians, it is not surprising that both have used athletics so often in their fiction, for sport so largely influences the American ethos and outlook. Especially in recent years, "sports in American fiction have served as a focal point for the examination of social or personal values,"[21] and these authors' books are among the best examples. Like their treatment of the other subsidiary themes discussed in this chapter—money, vocation, and the role of the clergy—their handling of sport sheds light on the present moment in this country.

6

Modus Operandi: The Literary Method
of Roth and Updike

ALTHOUGH ROTH AND UPDIKE are both realists and have much in common, in some respects they approach the writing of fiction rather differently. This contrast is evident in certain areas of literary technique. Their dissimilar handling of narrative perspective and character types, for example, is one such divergence. While Updike focuses upon the individual in relation to society, Roth is mainly concerned with depicting the individual's personal, inner-directed anguish. Moreover, he almost always portrays a particular "type"—the sophisticated, urbane, Jewish-American intellectual. Even Neil Klugman and Alexander Portnoy, who are not in fact writers or academicians, think and speak as if they were. Neil, a librarian, and Portnoy, a high-ranking liberal bureaucrat, share the bookishness and glib articulateness of Roth's actual literati: Gabe Wallach, Peter Tarnopol, David Kepesh, and Nathan Zuckerman. Neil, a former philosophy major, is described by Mr. Patimkin as "a student or something like that" (p. 105), while Portnoy has edited the Columbia Law Review, and is familiar with the work of Dos Passos, Freud, Kafka, Yeats, Dylan Thomas, and others. All of Roth's major novels concern the agonized soul-searchings of self-engrossed but highly intelligent protagonists who attempt to reconcile the conflicting demands of body and spirit, head and heart. Accordingly, Roth's fictions are often presented as the case record or end product of the narrator-protagonist's selfcontemplation. It is no accident, for example, that Portnoy, Tarnopol, Kepesh, and Zuckerman are all in analysis; the novels in which they appear are in effect the transcripts of their psychological struggles. Quite naturally, then, Roth in his "serious" works has tended to favor the first person participatory point of view.

Except for *When She Was Good, Zuckerman Unbound,* and *The Anatomy Lesson,* Roth's novels all employ first-person narrator-protagonists. Conversely, though, the bulk of his short stories are told from a third person omniscient perspective. But this is not as inconsistent as it may initially appear. To begin with, Roth has published only nineteen stories in all, more than half of them at the outset of his career, before 1960. Of the nine stories since then, one ("On the Air") is highly experimental, while two others ("The Good Girl" and "The Psychoanalytic Special") feature a female protagonist, both factors that might discourage first person treatment. Of the six remaining stories, half—"The Mistaken" (a forerunner to *Portnoy's Complaint*), "Courting Disaster," and the excellent ". . . Looking at Kafka,"—employ the first person participatory point of view, the narrative perspective that Roth clearly prefers.

The relative advantages and disadvantages of this particular mode of narration are well known. Most obviously, it permits total access to the inner workings of the central character's mind, and what is lost in "veracity" or "accuracy" is compensated for by the insights that are afforded into the protagonist's personality. That Portnoy, for example, is guilty of certain confusions and delusions is not a problem. Indeed, the very *raison d'être* of *Portnoy's Complaint* is to explore Portnoy's lack of self-knowledge; his fretful introspection and vitriolic outbursts are not only tangible evidence of his "complaint," but constitute the most direct possible articulation of it. Although an "unreliable narrator," he is such because of the very disorientation that makes his case exemplary and worthy of book-length documentation. The same might be said of Tarnopol, Kepesh, or—to a lesser extent—Zuckerman in *The Ghost Writer.*

What might be seen as something of a drawback to Roth's habitual use of first person narration, however, is a certain stridency to which more than a few critics have objected. Until recently there has been little distance between Roth's narrators and the events they describe, and his books have therefore exhibited an archly self-justifying tone. If Portnoy objects to what he imagines as the Jews' "sucking and sucking on that sour grape of a religion" (p. 76), a similar charge of obsessiveness could easily be leveled against him and the other Rothian narrators. Although they maintain a tone of mocking, self-righteous condescension, at times they appear almost morbidly preoccupied with their individual trials. The critics assailed this tendency even in Roth's early works, accusing Neil Klugman and Gabe Wallach of an overly-insistent proclamation of their own importance. And Portnoy and Tarnopol, of course, have been repeatedly indicted on similar charges.

Nevertheless, the protagonists' self-righteousness does not really create major difficulties, for in various ways Roth takes pains to offset it. In *Goodbye, Columbus,* for example, Neil's pose of moral superiority is shaken somewhat by his equally apparent feelings of social inferiority, and the humorous effects that inform the narrative. In *Letting Go,* Roth periodically provides lengthy "breaks" in Gabe's narration by interspersing sections of third person authorial narration that shift the focus from Gabe to the other characters. In *Portnoy's Complaint,* the uproariously comic treatment that Portnoy accords his plight tends to qualify his anger; D. Keith Mano has suggested that even Roth's sentence structure effaces Portnoy.[1] Only in *My Life as a Man* does the narrative voice really cloy. But the heavily autobiographical *Life* can be seen as a necessary, cathartic warming-up exercise in preparation for *The Professor of Desire* and the "Zuckerman" novels, Roth's most mature and tightly controlled books.

In *The Professor of Desire,* Roth mitigates the narrator's potentially obstructive self-centeredness simply by making him a highly appealing character. David Kepesh is far deeper than any previous Rothian narrator; his studied self-absorption, though typically obsessive, is counter balanced by a genuine sensitivity and fineness of response. In *The Ghost Writer* (as in the "Salad Days" section of *My Life as a Man*), retrospection serves to temper the narrator's self-importance, permitting a degree of ironic deflation that Roth's other narrators exercise far less well. *Zuckerman Unbound,* of course, solves the problem by means of its third person perspective, but also through the presence of Alvin Pepler. By inserting two long scenes that focus almost exclusively on the colorful Pepler, Zuckerman's "Conradian double," Roth creates some distance from Zuckerman, thus ensuring greater objectivity and preventing the protagonist from becoming too monopolistic. Such a strategy was not only clever but almost necessary to this book, for as Zuckerman admits, the inconveniences of great wealth do not constitute a topic likely to elicit much sympathy. But *Zuckerman Unbound* (like its sequel,

The Anatomy Lesson) is atypical. Usually Roth employs the first person perspective in keeping with the current preference for confessional effects, a trend that Roth himself has played a considerable part in creating and perpetuating, especially through *Portnoy's Complaint.*

What is most significant, perhaps, is that Roth's repeated use of highly subjective, protagonist-centered narration may well be linked to the fact that ethnicity is so central in his work. Even in *My Life as a Man* and *The Professor of Desire,* books in which ethnic identity is not an ostensibly major issue, his protagonists are nevertheless quite conscious of their Jewishness, and Roth clearly wishes us to see this as contributing to their anxiety. Roth has said that he understands "what Leslie Fiedler said about a Jew being—not perhaps an exile, but an outsider. If I can make any sense about my Jewishness and of my desire to . . . call myself a Jew, it is in terms of my outsideness in the general assumptions of American culture."[2] Accordingly, the typical Rothian protagonist, regardless of whatever social prominence he may enjoy, exists in a state of cultural isolation; his insularity is partially a result not only of whatever psychological difficulties he may be experiencing, but also of the Jews' still somewhat marginal position in American society. This, coupled with what Stanley Cooperman calls the "'talent for suffering,' that anguished, self-lacerating moral judgment which is in essence Judaic,"[3] dictates that he must ultimately rely on the strength of his own inner resources, his own ability to achieve perspective. Small wonder, then, that Roth's fictions are so invariably couched in the voices of his protagonists; indeed, one might even say that the fictions and the protagonists are one, that beyond the protagonists themselves, little else matters in his fictional universe.

Not so with Updike, whose novels reflect a rather quaintly conventional concern with human interrelationships. Robert Detweiler has concisely summarized the essential contrast between Updike's perspective and Roth's: "there is a fundamental difference between the two. Updike writes of relationships (in the plural) and describes connections between individuals and natural and social institutions as symptomatic of the individual and societal search for God. Roth writes of relationship (in the singular) as both the method of and the place for finding ultimate meaning."[4] Accordingly, Updike's approach to narration is the opposite of Roth's. Nearly all of Updike's novels and more than three-fourths of his numerous short stories employ the third person authorial voice, a narrative perspective whose quality of comprehensive, "objective" omniscience is well suited to his purposes. Congruently, Updike's protagonists tend to be far more diverse than Roth's. While Roth repeatedly works with one basic character type, Updike's protagonists can be seen as falling into three main categories: the small-town adolescent boy, typified by Peter Caldwell of *The Centaur,* and the variously-named youths of the "Olinger" stories; the "swinging," upper middle class sophisticate of W.A.S.P. suburbia, such as Joey Robinson of *Of the Farm,* Piet Hanema of *Couples,* Jerry Conant of *Marry Me,* Richard Maple of the "Maples" stories, and even the Reverend Mr. Marshfield of *A Month of Sundays;* and, perhaps most importantly, the "working class hero" of the "Rabbit" novels, Harry Angstrom.

Of course, there are exceptions to all of this, which even a casual review of both writers' work will readily bring to light. Roth's female protagonists, Lucy Nelson of *When She Was Good,* Ella Wittig of "The Psychoanalytic Special," and Laurie Bowen of "The Good Girl," for example, are clearly anomalous, as is the fact that these works employ a third person omniscient perspective. Similarly, Word Smith of *The Great American Novel* is in no way representative of Roth's first-person narrators. And it would be difficult indeed to see John Hook of *The Poorhouse Fair* or Henry Bech as belonging to any of the Updikean character types suggested here. Further, the first-person perspective of *A Month of Sundays* and *Of the Farm* is also a variation on Updike's usual method in his longer works, just as *Zuckerman Unbound* and *The Anatomy Lesson* are a departure from Roth's customary first-person approach. Nevertheless, these generalizations are usually reliable when applied to the two writers' most representative fiction.

What warrants further comment is Updike's perspective in the "Rabbit" novels. To say simply that these books are "third-person omniscient" narratives would be to overlook an important source of their special appeal. Although Rabbit's ongoing saga is indeed told from a *technically* omniscient point of view, the narrative voice is clearly a blend of both Rabbit's and the author's. Once these novels are underway, a very deliberate and remarkably well-controlled interweaving of voices begins to occur, as Updike achieves a bitonal quality that enables him to exploit the advantages of both first and third person narration. The following passage, from *Rabbit Is Rich,* is typical:

Houses of sandstone. A billboard pointing to a natural cave. He wonders who goes there anymore, natural caves a thing of the past, like waterfalls. Men in straw hats. Women with not even their ankles showing. Natural wonders. That smartass young female announcer—he hasn't heard her for a while, he thought maybe the station had fired her, too sassy or got pregnant—comes on and says that the Pope has addressed the UN and is stopping in Harlem on his way to Yankee Stadium. Harry saw the cocky little guy on television last night, getting soaked in Boston in his white robes, you had to admire his English, about his seventh language, and who was the deadpan guy standing there holding the umbrella over him? Some Vatican bigwig, but Pru didn't seem to know any more than he did, what's the good of being raised a Catholic? In Europe, gold rose today to a new high of four hundred forty-four dollars an ounce while the dollar slipped to new lows. The station fades and returns as the road twists among the hilly fields. Harry calculates, up eighty dollars in less than three weeks, thirty times eighty is two thousand four hundred, when you're rich you get richer, just like Pop used to say. In some of the fields the corn stands tall, others are stubble. He glides through the ugly string town of Galilee, on the lookout for the orange Corolla. (pp. 275–76)

Although the events described here are obviously presented in the third person, the implied value judgments are clearly Rabbit's own, as is much of the diction. Indeed, whole sentences must be read as Rabbit's although Updike purposely omits quotation marks and attributing phrases. The result is a clever sort of literary pointillism, which, reinforced by Updike's choice of the historical present tense, creates a sense of verisimilitude without sacrificing the obvious stylistic advantages of third person viewpoint. This is especially important to the success of the "Rabbit" novels, for Harry (unlike Roth's protagonists) is simply too uncultivated and nonverbal to serve as an effective narrator strictly on his own. Through this delicate balancing of voices—sometimes called the "free indirect style" of narration—Updike is able to reveal character by giving Harry his say, while still maintaining a polished effect and the privileges of omniscience.

Thus, Updike can exercise his stylistic agility without violating the "givens" of the fictional world he has chosen to represent. Of course, this is also a question of language and style, an area which is of considerable interest to any discussion of Roth and Updike; both writers are often applauded for their skill with language, and each possesses a highly dis-

tinctive voice. As with certain other aspects of these writers'
work, however, they differ greatly with regard to the stylistic
component. While Roth's language is predominantly conversational—direct, uncluttered, and colloquial—Updike's
is noted for its traditionally "literary" inclination. Where
Roth favors the pungent, sharp-edged word or phrase, Updike generally chooses the more ornately formal locution. In
addition, Roth tends more toward exposition, while Updike
is given to frequent passages of detailed description, coupled
with lengthy flights of metaphorical allusion. Certainly, this
disparity is closely linked to the two writers' differing prefer-
ences regarding narrative perspective. In Roth's work, the
narrator-protagonist is primarily concerned with telling his
own story, and in his own words, while Updike's fiction is
usually channeled through a third person authorial monitor
that places the protagonist in a broader context.

Of course, qualifications are in order here. Roth is a highly
deliberate stylist whose quality of seeming spontaneity is actually the result of an entirely conscious design. Similarly,
Updike often ventures into Rothian colloquialism, abandoning his usual highflown, embroidered prose to embrace a
more vernacular mode of expression, especially, for example,
when paraphrasing Harry Angstrom's numerous internal
monologues or reporting Harry's remarks. Moreover, these
writers have certain stylistic affinities. Both freely employ the
explicit "vulgarisms" of contemporary American English, a
tendency that underscores their shared preference for realistic dialogue. And both have experimented with highly uncharacteristic narrative voices, Roth in *When She Was Good,
The Great American Novel,* and *Our Gang,* and Updike in *A
Month of Sundays, The Coup,* and certain short stories. For the
most part, though, the basic differences outlined above are

real ones, and no attentive reader would be likely to confuse characteristic samplings of these writers' prose.

Certainly, Roth's style typifies that blend of toughness and elegance that has been termed the "Jewish-American" manner of writing. In *World of Our Fathers,* Irving Howe remarks upon the impressive range that this style embraces, as it incorporates influences "from the high gravity of Yiddish declamation to the gutter sparklings of the street." He describes Saul Bellow's writing as the culmination of the Jewish-American literary tradition:

Bellow's style draws upon Yiddish, not so much through borrowed diction as through underlying intonation and rhythm. The jabbing interchange of ironies, the intimate vulgarities, the blend of sardonic and sentimental which characterizes Yiddish speech . . . what emerges is . . . a vibrant linguistic transmutation. . . . Bellow has brought to completion the first major new style in American prose fiction since those of Hemingway and Faulkner: a mingling of high-flown intellectual bravado with racy-tough street Jewishness, all in a comic rhetoric that keeps turning its head back toward Yiddish even as it keeps racing away from it. And throughout his work there is a half-mocking voice . . . self-puncturing, so that his relation to the materials of immigrant life always remains quizzical and probing.[5]

These qualities are observable in Roth's work, as well, and Roth himself has commented at length on the question of the Jewish-American style, responding to Harvey Swados's description of it as "a nervous muscular prose . . . a kind of prose poetry":

When writers who do not feel much of a connection to Lord Chesterfield begin to realize that they are under no real obligation to try and write like that distinguished old stylist, they are likely enough to go out and be bouncy. Also, there is the matter of the spoken language which these writers have heard, as our statesmen might put it, in the schools, the homes, the churches and the synagogues of the nation. I would even say that when the bouncy style is not an attempt to dazzle the reader, or one's self, but to incorporate . . . nuances, and emphases of urban and immigrant speech, the result can sometimes be a language of new and rich emotional subtleties, with a kind of back-handed charm and irony all its own.[6]

What Roth does not mention here is that this attempt to capture the rhythms of spoken American English is not without precedent. Jewish-American literature (and Roth's work in particular) is solidly in the American vernacular tradition. *Portnoy's Complaint* can even be viewed as a legitimate literary descendant of Twain's *Huckleberry Finn,* the first American literary masterpiece to use an exclusively first person colloquial idiom. Roth takes his place alongside Twain and such other American masters of the colloquial style as Lewis, Lardner, Gertrude Stein, and Hemingway. But it would be quite mistaken to suppose that Roth's fondness for the actual rhythms of the spoken idiom, and his apparent ease of composition are somehow indicative of a facile reliance on mere slapdash transcription. Roth is very much aware of the subtleties of usage, as revealed by his comments on *When She Was Good* and *Our Gang.* Like *Portnoy's Complaint,* both works in part attempt to capture and lampoon certain kinds of speech. In the former, Roth seeks to reinforce the stultification and self-deception that so deaden his characters' lives, by faithfully reproducing the blandness and sterility of their accustomed habits of conversation. Similarly, Roth's overt burlesque of Nixonian rhetoric on *Our Gang* results in another work in which, to some extent, "the medium is the message." Roth has spoken on these matters: "there was a time when I . . . associated the rhetoric employed by the heroine of

When She Was Good to disguise from herself her vengeful de-
structiveness with the kind of language our government used
when they spoke of 'saving' the Vietnamese by means of sys-
tematic annihilation."[7] Elsewhere he has said, "I've been attracted to prose that has the turns, vibrations, intonations,
and cadences, the spontaneity and ease, of spoken language,
at the same time that it is solidly grounded on the page,
weighted with the irony, precision, and ambiguity associated
with a more traditional literary rhetoric."[8] Like any good
stylist, then, Roth achieves his effects consciously, through
craft, and his novels and stories abound with examples of his
stylistic virtuosity.

Perhaps the most sensitive and thorough treatment of Roth's
style is "About Portnoy," by Patricia Meyer Spacks, who
cites the highly accomplished tonal manipulation which, even
more than the novel's subject matter, accounts for its special
"personality." She stresses the very conscious stylistic awareness that underlies the book's illusion of extemporaneity. The
novel is, she says, "shaped by style. . . . its language . . . at
times is identical with its substance." By this she means that
the phraseology, the tempo of the sentences, and the choice of
words reinforce the sense of comic incongruity that is so central a feature of the book. The novel's tone is carefully manip-
ulated through language, as Roth selects a mode of expression that "enforces the reader's consciousness of the
ludicrous with its incongruous conjunctions, its comic restoration of literal force to dead metaphor." Most importantly,
however, Roth exercises a highly "literary" control over
Portnoy's street-wise ideolect. "The calculated rhythms and
ironies, the tonal mixture . . . even the punctuation,"
Spacks says, "all suggest the formalities of written rather
than oral communication. . . . the freedom of spoken language . . . combines with the control of the written form."[9]

Lately, several critics—Anatole Broyard, Judith Yaross Lee, G. W. Ireland—have applauded Roth's very individualized "voice," and Joseph Podhoretz has asserted that "Roth writes an English sentence better than . . . anyone else alive."[10] Nevertheless, Roth's conscious stylistic artistry is an aspect of his craft that has been largely overlooked and undervalued.

Ironically, quite the opposite is true in Updike's case. Virtually all of the critics acknowledge his stylistic flair, and some actually cite this aspect of his work in order to denigrate him. They claim that his verbal facility is his only virtue, as if his flights of language constituted an attempt to get by on dazzle. Certain critics, notably Richard Gilman and Norman Podhoretz, have charged that Updike's style is overblown, forced, and cumbersomely ornate. These indictments are justified only to a very limited extent. Upon occasion (especially in early works), Updike's rhetoric does in fact become obtrusive. Certain passages from *The Poorhouse Fair* (too heavily influenced by Faulkner and Wolfe) are especially so. But such instances are rare. As a rule, Updike is very much in control, maintaining a highly polished stylistic brilliance that—far from becoming counterproductive—is quite well suited to his purposes, enabling him to invest his rather commonplace subject matter with fresh vitality.

If Updike is a chronicler of the everyday, his rendition of this "middleness" never becomes itself middling; through his use of language, he both elevates and transcends his material, adroitly reawakening the reader to life's small wonders by creating striking new perspectives. For the most part, this sharpness of perception is achieved by virtue of the extreme specificity that invests Updike's presentation of physical detail. Equally central to Updike's method, however, is his selectivity in choosing vivid (often onomatopoeic) verbs and unusual but precise modifers. Moreover, Updike's descriptions do not rely exclusively on visual detail. Although there is a great deal of that, there is also considerable emphasis on *other* sensory impressions, as well: the tactile, the auditory, the olfactory. Updike records the moment in a very total way, drawing the reader into a feeling almost of participation in the events described.

Robert Detweiler has suggested that Updike's metaphors are akin to those of the metaphysical poets, demonstrating an "elegant control of the delicate tension between the tangible and the fanciful."[11] The comparison is apt; repeatedly, the reader is struck by the simultaneous oddity and appropriateness of Updike's images, remarkably original figures of speech that evoke vivid mental pictures while also affording new perceptions of the external world. This metaphoric inventiveness characterizes all of Updike's work, and his corpus abounds with memorable examples. In the interest of concision, though, a few will suffice:

The green hay turned greasy in tone as the cloudlets, one by one, dipped it in shadow, and the sky behind the woods acquired the sullen solid pitch that wallpapers long hidden behind a sofa reveal to the movers.

(Of the Farm, p. 63)

Whatever he expects when he flicks on the inside hall light, it is not the same old furniture, the fake cobbler's bench, the sofa and the silverthread chair facing each other like two bulky drunks too tired to go upstairs.

(Rabbit Redux, pp. 140–41)

Seeing the collision coming, Harry expected it to happen in slow motion, like on television, but instead it happened comically fast, like two dogs tangling and then thinking better of it.

(Rabbit Is Rich, p. 170)

Such originality is rare indeed. But so, too, is Updike's background unusual. Not only is he unique among major contemporary American novelists in being a successful poet as well, but he has also entertained a lifelong interest in art, having spent a postgraduate year (1954–55) on a Knox Fellowship at Oxford's Ruskin School of Drawing and Fine Arts. These experiences have obviously been instrumental in fostering the individuality of Updike's style. Like Hemingway, who claimed to have learned much from Cezanne, Updike has been greatly influenced by his knowledge of painting and illustration, and his easy familiarity with the principles of versification also contributes to the tenor of his writing. A highly pictorial quality informs his work, combining with an acute sensitivity to the patterns and nuances of language, to create a style that is unmistakable in its precision and beauty.

In Updike's fiction—particularly the "Olinger" works and the "Rabbit" novels—setting is also vitally important. As Tony Tanner has observed, "Updike's work is . . . deeply rooted in his own . . . territorial experience."[12] But in Roth's case, setting functions secondarily. Only in *Goodbye, Columbus, Portnoy's Complaint,* and *Zuckerman Unbound* is it at all significant. And even in those books, Roth's fictional landscape is primarily that of the mind; his protagonists live their lives and endure their torments in a psychological world largely of their own making. But this is not to imply that Roth's fictions occur on an empty stage. Among Roth's most highly developed skills is his ability to vividly evoke a sense of the physical surroundings within which his characters act out their personal dramas.

Nevertheless, there is an essential difference between Roth's and Updike's use of setting. Whereas Updike describes minutely, rendering every detail, thereby conveying a sense of place almost for its own sake, Roth's evocation of detail is quite selective. Although Roth will often create a sharply visual representation and invest it with discrete particularity, he does so primarily to advance characterization. Like Fitzgerald, he compares, contrasts, and otherwise juxtaposes his characters' homes, neighborhoods, offices, vehicles, et cetera, mainly for the purpose of revealing and delineating their personalities. The details of downtown Woodenton in "Eli, the Fanatic," for example, are less important in themselves than as outward indices of a particular lifestyle. Likewise, in *Portnoy's Complaint,* the hypergentile quality of the Pumpkin's Iowa heartland and, say, the exclusively Jewish character of Israel or of the old neighborhood in Newark are purposely depicted—but primarily for the sake of revealing Portnoy's responses to them. Indeed, examples of Roth's manipulation of setting abound. Interiors, particularly, function significantly in his work. We need only to recall Uncle Asher's fetid studio in *Letting Go,* the Kepeshes' homey resort hotel in *The Professor of Desire,* or Lonoff's New England home in *The Ghost Writer,* to see how this is so.

One further point should be made in this context. As the Jewish-American experience that Roth characteristically portrays is basically an urban one, his fiction, like that of most Jewish-American writers, reflects that fact. Almost all of his novels and stories take place in urban settings, in cities such as Newark, Jersey City, Camden, Chicago, and New York. Although Roth and Updike depict both the urban fleshpot and "the good remembered town" (Updike's phrase, from the early poem "Shillington"), in Roth's case they are one and the same, the only difference being that which exists in the protagonist's mind, depending mainly upon his age at the time of the events in question. Even when Roth ventures into suburbia in his fiction—as in *Goodbye, Columbus* and "Eli, the Fanatic"—he does so not to "settle down," but only to "visit," and always returns with the suggestion that there is something either sterile and corrupting, or falsely attractive about that environment. This implication is present, too, in *The Professor of Desire,* when Kepesh views his idyllic summer retreat as symbolic of a temporary happiness that cannot last. And in *The Ghost Writer,* Zuckerman learns that although Lonoff's remote country residence seems to be a cozy retreat, it is actually part of the older man's self-constructed prison of isolation.

The city is the Rothian protagonist's true métier, as virtually every one of Roth's novels demonstrates. Neil Klugman, for example, says, "I felt a deep knowledge of Newark, an attachment so rooted that it could not help but branch out into affection" (p. 41), and we are reminded of Portnoy's loving reminiscences of childhood visits to the *shvitz* baths with his father, and of Sunday morning softball games involving the Jewish men of Jersey City and Newark. Nevertheless, these are paeans for a distinctly Jewish urban experience, one that depends for its substance not upon any particular urban location, but which presupposes membership in a particular ethnic group. Significantly, Zuckerman's Newark is portrayed in *The Anatomy Lesson* as no longer viable because it is "occupied now by an alien tribe."[13] Repeatedly, the emphasis falls not so much upon physical surroundings themselves, but upon states of mind. Conversely, Updike's work is inextricably linked to one specific area of the country. His characters and their geographical origins in fact define each other. This is hardly the case in Roth's fiction, where the characters' identities have been determined largely by their membership in a more far-flung, worldwide community. It is not surprising, then, that at crucial points in their lives, Portnoy, Gabe Wallach, Nathan Zuckerman, and David Kepesh all travel to Europe in an effort to define themselves.

Updike's fictional world is far narrower; his books are almost always set in southeastern Pennsylvania and the New England states. Repeatedly he has depicted his hometown, Shillington, and nearby Reading (as well as several other Pennsylvania towns: Bethlehem, Plowville, et al.), and although these places are nominally disguised as Olinger, Brewer, Galilee, and Firetown, the correspondences are apparent. Even in *The Poorhouse Fair,* ostensibly set in New Jersey, Updike is actually drawing upon memories of his early years in Shillington. In "The Dogwood Tree: A Boyhood," Updike says that near his home there was in fact a "County Home—an immense yellow poorhouse . . . surrounded by a sandstone wall,"[14] much like the institution in the novel. Moreover, specific Reading-Shillington landmarks, such as Mt. Penn, the Bachman Pretzel Co., and the Luden's coughdrop factory, appear reincarnated in the fiction as Mt. Judge, the Owl Pretzel Co., and the Essick's coughdrop factory.

Granted, Updike has occasionally used various other settings—New England, New York City, Europe, and even Africa—but most of his best work to date has been that which focuses on the Olinger-Brewer environs. Moreover, even in the suburban works there is in the recurring theme of lost innocence an implied yearning for the simpler world of the Pennsylvania Dutch country. The previously mentioned early poem "Shillington" embodies Updike's continuing preoccupation with the idea that, in Thomas Wolfe's familiar phrase, we "can never go home again," but always yearn to: "We have one home, the first, and leave that one. / The having and leaving go on together."[15]

Indeed, Updike has described the town of Shillington as "a calm point that in my subjective geography is still the center of the world."[16] He has explained that "I am drawn to southeastern Pennsylvania because I know how things happen there, or at least how they used to happen. Once you have in your bones the fundamental feasibilities of a place, you can imagine there freely."[17] Not surprisingly, his "Olinger" fictions and the "Rabbit" novels possess the ring of truth, which the suburban fictions sometimes lack. Like Cheever's Wapshot or Faulkner's "little postage stamp of native soil," Yoknapatawpha County, Updike's version of southeast Pennsylvania is an imaginary one, but has its model in actuality. He focuses on his particular part of the Keystone state not to cultivate a narrow parochialism, but to delineate an area of the country that he considers typical. In *Rabbit Redux,* a newspaper headline blares, "BREWER MIDDLE AMERICA? *Gotham Filmmakers Think So*" (p. 183) in announcing that Harry Angstrom's hometown has been selected as the location of an upcoming movie. Obviously, Updike believes that his section of the country is representative, and has called Reading "to me . . . the master of cities, the one at the center that all others echo."[18] Although the Brewer-Olinger setting seems on first glance rather restricted and local, it becomes, when magnified and compounded, an exemplary one, symbolic of midtwentieth century W.A.S.P. America at large.

If Updike's intention is to show "the American Protestant small-town middle class,"[19] his choice of Reading as his fictional locale is entirely appropriate. A once prosperous but now decaying industrial town, Reading is typical of many small American cities. In *The Centaur* Updike places Reading (there called Alton—i.e., "all-town") at the heart of "the great Middle Atlantic civilization" (p. 145), comparing it to other factory towns: Altoona and Hagerstown in Pennsylvania; Bridgeport and New Haven in Connecticut; Binghamton, Johnstown, and Elmira in New York; Trenton, New Jersey; and Wheeling, West Virginia. In short, Updike's use of setting is purposeful, as he presents a microcosm which in its typicality becomes emblematic of the entire way of life that he wishes to record.

Another interesting area of commonality between Roth and Updike is their mutual use of symbolism. Both are accomplished in the manipulation of this device, and have applied it skillfully in some of their best works. The symbols that these writers create are never farfetched or contrived, but are organic, growing out of the fundamental imperatives of the works in which they appear, rather like the "practical" or "natural" symbols of Hemingway: significant points of personal appearance, physical surroundings, or the like, which contribute powerfully to the effectiveness of a scene. We are reminded, for example, of the numerous references to the "heart" that appear throughout Roth's *Letting Go,* functioning on both the realistic and metaphoric levels, as do the many allusions to apples in *The Professor of Desire.* But it is in his early work, principally in the novella and the short stories of *Goodbye, Columbus,* that Roth makes his most intensive use of symbolism. In these works, Roth repeatedly amplifies the meaning of the literal events by subtly introducing symbolic elements that reinforce and expand the significance of the surface action.

In the novella, especially, symbols abound, and the title itself is significant in this regard. Although on one level "Goodbye, Columbus" is simply an allusion to the melodramatic Ohio State phonograph record that Ron Patimkin so nostalgically cherishes, the valediction also evokes "the Yiddish curse '*A klug af Columbus!*' (A curse on Columbus!) which was a commonplace of the Lower East Side's nongolden streets."[20] Although the "New World" of affluent Jewish suburbia is initially attractive to Neil Klugman, he ultimately rejects it, and the cultural disparity between that environment and his own "Old world" neighborhood in Newark is among the book's primary tensions. This theme is introduced early in the novella, and is embodied in Neil's Aunt Gladys, who serves to heighten the contrast between the opulence of the Patimkins' milieu and the practical, self-sacrificing ambience of the immigrant homelife of which Neil is a product. With her readily identifiable Yiddish-American speech patterns and her relentlessly pragmatic emphasis on such everyday concerns as food and other domestic considerations, she is the embodiment of the kvetching wife and mother of so many Jewish jokes. Her remoteness from the Patimkins is succinctly symbolized by the strictly utilitarian function served by her suburban telephone directory, which is used to support a sagging dresser.

But there is abundant evidence that Neil, despite his stance of self-righteous moral superiority, is initially rather fascinated by the Patimkins and their wealth, and he seems to enjoy the role of social climber. As we have seen, the suburban "paradise" of Short Hills is frequently described in highly symbolic terms that liken it to an Edenic or heavenly realm. Neil's enthrallment with suburbia is expressed in his frequent comments to the effect that its physical setting is preferable to that of Newark. Repeatedly he mentions the cooler air, the mountains, the rolling lawns—that is, the natural beauty—of Short Hills. Fittingly, his first date with Brenda takes place in a small park, where the girl plays tennis. To partake of these Edenic surroundings, however, one must have money, and the ironic union of natural and material abundance is embodied in the wry image of the "sporting goods trees" that adorn the Patimkins' yard: "Outside, through the wide picture window, I could see the back lawn with its twin oak trees. I say oaks, though fancifully, one might call them sporting-goods trees. Beneath their branches, like fruit dropped from their limbs, were two irons, a golf ball, a tennis can, a base-ball bat, basketball, a first-baseman's glove, and what was apparently a riding crop" (pp. 31–32).

Later, when describing Newark's formerly Jewish Third Ward, Neil observes that "on the streets, instead of Yiddish, one heard the shouts of Negro children playing at Willie Mays with a broom handle and half a rubber ball. The neighborhood had changed." (p. 101). The reference to stickball creates a contrast with the games enjoyed by the Patimkins. While their sports require expensive equipment of the type yielded by the "sporting-goods tree," stickball is played with a broom handle and an inexpensive rubber ball. Moreover, Roth depicts here a specifically urban version of stickball in which the ball is deliberately cut in half so that it will be less likely to travel great distances and become lost on the teeming city streets. Thus Roth uses sports imagery adroitly to heighten the sense of disparity between suburbia and the inner city. In addition, the mention of the black children and the black baseball star Willie Mays (as opposed to the Patimkins' idol, Mickey Mantle) and the fact that "Negroes were making the same migration, following the steps of the Jews" (p. 101) serve to link Neil symbolically with the blacks, for Neil is basically a Newarker at heart, and he clearly resents Brenda's slighting attitude toward the city. Roth establishes a very definite link between Neil and the blacks. Twice, for example, Neil mentally aligns himself with Carlota, the Patimkins' maid: "For a while I remained in the hall, bitten with the urge to slide quietly out of the house, into my car, and back to Newark. . . . I felt like Carlota; no, not even as comfortable as that." (p. 50); "I said hello to her as I went out the back door, and though she did not return the greeting, I felt a kinship with one who, like me, had been partially wooed and won on Patimkin fruit" (p. 88). The idea, of course, is that

Neil is an outsider in the Patimkins' realm. As a representative of "Old World" Newark, he is socially unacceptable to them, a minority within a minority, his own inner conviction of personal worthiness notwithstanding.

This pattern of racial-ethnic symbolism finds its fullest expression in Neil's relationship with the young black boy who visits the Newark Library to admire the Gauguin reproductions. It is not accidental that Neil describes Brenda as "a sailor's dream of a Polynesian maiden" (p. 25), and that the black lad is attracted by Gauguin's paintings of native women. The parallel becomes explicit when Neil refers to Short Hills as "in my mind's eye, at dusk, rose-colored, like a Gauguin stream" (p. 48). The symbolism is apparent; both the boy and Neil yearn for a "higher version" of their respective ethnic situations. The boy expresses his desire to escape the black ghetto for Gauguin's island paradise when he asks, "That ain't no place you could go, is it? Like a ree-*sort*?" (p. 47). Similarly, Neil desires to flee the Jewish ghetto for Short Hills, and does, in fact, spend his two-week vacation there. Moreover, just as Neil refers calculatingly to the "lousy hundred and eighty feet that make summer nights so much cooler in Short Hills than they are in Newark" (p. 24), the child seems at one point to be "counting the number of marble stairs" (p. 43) that lead out of the ghetto to Stack Three and the "heart" section (a significant, even if unintentional, pun, in view of the Yiddish proverb that Roth has chosen as the epigraph of the book: "The heart is half a prophet").

There is still another parallel between Neil and the boy, in that each denigrates his roots. Just as Neil disdains "Old World" Jewishness, the boy reveals his belief that Gauguin "don't *take* pictures like no colored man would. He's a good

picture taker" (pp. 47-48). As Norman Leer points out,
"The symbols of the Columbus record, the South Seas island, and the Negro boy are brought together in a dream that
Neil has one night as he sleeps beside Brenda."[21] In the
dream, the boy and Neil are forced to sail unwillingly away
from the island, as the maidens bid them "Goodbye, Columbus." This presages the plot developments that follow. The
boy's Gauguin book (which he is unable, because of social
circumstances, to take home) is withdrawn by someone else,
and Brenda (whom Neil, also because of social circumstances, is unable to really "possess") departs for Radcliffe.
Neil, as yet unaware that his relationship with Brenda is at an
end, ironically speculates that the black boy has "given up on
the library and gone back to playing Willie Mays in the
streets. He was better off. . . . No sense carrying dreams of
Tahiti in your head, if you can't afford the fare" (pp. 131-32).
When the romance is terminated immediately thereafter, the
parallel between Neil and the boy is completely established.
Upon leaving Brenda for the last time, Neil stares resentfully
at Harvard's Lamont Library—symbolic, of course, of the
world of privilege in which Brenda moves, and contrasted as
such with the Newark Public Library in which Neil works
and the boy browses. Thus, the novella's various tropes are
brought full circle.

Although it has received comparatively little critical analysis, the short story "Epstein" also utilizes symbolic detail
adroitly, and therefore merits fuller examination here. For
instance, the otherwise inconsequential fact that Sheila Epstein's boyfriend, Marvin, is "chinless" (p. 218) takes on importance when we learn that the Epstein family physiognomy
is characterized by a "strong chin" (p. 219). The sonless Epstein is depressed by the prospect of his business possibly

passing into Marvin's hands, and the minor aspect of the youth's appearance serves to reinforce Epstein's disappointment by symbolizing the fact that Marvin is not "family."

When Epstein first meets Ida Kaufman, his lover, he is immediately ticketed by a policeman for failing to observe "a red light which, in his joy, he had not seen. It was the first of three tickets he received that day . . . . as he told Ida, when you're laughing so hard you have tears in your eyes, how can you tell the green lights from the red ones, fast from slow?" (p. 225) The tickets are, as one critic has observed, "a foreshadowing of things to come," symbols of "society's disapproval."[22] This device reappears at the end of the story when Epstein, having suffered a heart attack during coitus, is carried away in the ambulance, which has a red light slowly spinning on its roof.

Appropriately, Epstein's affair had begun on a Monday morning in April, "the cruellest month." The warm spring weather has reawakened Epstein's sexual urges, and the day is described in phallic terms: "The sun glinted in the sky like a young athlete's trophy" (p. 223). But after Epstein's heart attack, a very different phallic symbol appears: "His tongue hung over his teeth like a dead snake" (p. 243). And Epstein's defeat is reflected by the events in his kitchen as the ambulance approaches: "The wail grew louder. 'God,' Sheila said, 'it sounds like the end of the world.' And Marvin, who had been polishing his guitar with a red handkerchief, immediately broke into song, a high-pitched, shut-eyed Negro tune about the end of the world" (p. 239). For Epstein, "the end of the world" has in fact arrived, for his desperate attempt to make, in Roth's words, "a final struggle" against "exhaustion, decay and disappointment"[23] has been thwarted. Unlike Malamud's Levin, he is simply too old to forge a "new life." In attempting to regain happiness through sexual reinvolvement, Epstein tends to emphasize youth, dwelling upon his own younger days, and referring to his twenty-two-year-old nephew as being only twenty. Epstein wishes to turn back the clock; but society, symbolized by the doctor who ministers to Epstein after his attack, emphasizes the cruel reality of aging. To Goldie's comment that Epstein has never before experienced heart trouble, the doctor replies " 'A man sixty, sixty-five, it happens. . . . ' 'He's only fifty-nine.' 'Some only,' the doctor said" (p. 243).

Clearly, Roth's use of symbolism in his early works contributes importantly to their total effect. The symbols in the *Goodbye, Columbus* volume are exemplary of Roth's ability to provide a substratum of metaphorical allusion and cross-reference that expands and enriches the realistic quality of the fiction without being contrived or intrusive. Updike, too, has demonstrated this facility; but in his oeuvre, symbolism is more pervasive. Although Updike is no less the realist than Roth, he is more the conscious symbolist. Perhaps his greater fondness for symbolic effects, and his continued use of them throughout his career, are attributable to his poetical inclinations. In addition to his novels and short story collections, Updike has published four volumes of verse. If his is not generally accorded the status of "serious" poetry—even *Midpoint*, his one self-proclaimed venture in that direction, has not met with much critical applause—it is clever, witty, and most entertaining, and its antic freshness is largely the result of Updike's ability to devise striking metaphors and symbols. This talent manifests itself with equal originality in his fiction.

Except in *The Centaur*, where the symbolic elements are deliberately superimposed upon the literal framework of the narrative, Updike's symbolism is generated from within his dramatic situations; like Roth, he always achieves a true inte-

gration between the literal and the figurative. Updike's fictitious author Henry Bech (to some extent, a persona) speaks
of his desire to "place beneath the melody of plot a counter-
melody of imagery,"[24] and Updike himself has remarked that
his "deepest pride" as an author is in his "ability to keep an
organized mass of images moving forward."[25]

Although symbolism is an important feature of virtually all
of Updike's novels and a great many of his short stories, it is
most extensively used in the "Rabbit" novels, where Harry
Angstrom's problems—although different in each of the
three books—are reflected in a variety of image patterns,
metaphors, and tropes. Entirely appropriate to Harry's situation, these devices never seem forced or strained, and therefore serve well the purpose of emphasizing Harry's difficulties. In this context, *Rabbit Redux* warrants extended commentary. Although not a better novel than *Rabbit, Run* or
Rabbit Is Rich, it is more ambitious in scope, and the symbol
patterns that inform it are accordingly more complicated.
The symbolism in *Rabbit, Run* (already quite amply explicat-
ed by Clinton S. Burhans and other critics) and in *Rabbit Is
Rich* accentuates those novels' concern with Harry's somewhat misdirected strivings—in the former novel, for spiritual
transcendence; in the latter, for worldly gain. But the dominant images of *Rabbit Redux* create an atmosphere of passive
immobility, of arrested and purposeless movement. Among
the multiple image patterns that function in this way to reinforce the novel's pervasive emphasis on lassitude and inertia
are the recurring references to coldness and frigidity, which
run throughout. Joyce Markle, the first critic to comment on
this particular feature of the book, has compiled a lengthy
catalog of such allusions, which, as she says, serve to convey
the idea that in a "demoralized society, emptied of belief

in anything, the characters are emotionally paralyzed—frozen."[26]

Updike introduces this motif at the outset of the novel, as Harry and his father leave work and pay their habitual visit to a nearby tavern. The brightness of the day gives the neighborhood the appearance of "a frozen explosion" (p. 3), the air-conditioned interior of the bar is uncomfortably cold, Harry orders frozen daiquiris, the television broadcasts an inane game show on which a flirtatious housewife wins "an eight-foot frozen-food locker" (p. 7), and Earl Angstrom figuratively suggests that Harry's ailing mother "stay in bed . . . . take care of herself, put herself in deep freeze" (p. 8) until a cure is developed for her Parkinson's Disease. Clearly, these repeated allusions function just as Markle suggests, to elicit a chilling aura of demoralization that is central to the entire scene. The brittle, tentative fencing that passes for conversation between the Angstrom men is lent an additional measure of discomfort by the almost tactile sensation of coldness that these references create.

This motif is but one of many, however, that are introduced in the barroom scene. The novel's opening pages also include a number of other references of a similarly disspiriting sort, which are related in various ways to the frigidity motif and to each other—allusions to promiscuity, artificiality, paleness, ghostliness, and death. In this sense, the opening tableau prefigures the method of the entire novel, which is built around an extremely complicated system of interlocking themes and symbolic tropes. The great complexity of the interrelationships among these multiple strands of symbolic reference can barely be suggested, because of the book's labyrinthine intricacy of cross-reference. Nevertheless, one recognizes here the novel's principal strength, for despite its seemingly Gordian convolutions, *Rabbit Redux* is a tightly structured object lesson in controlled imagistic virtuosity.

Referring to the role of myth and scripture in his work, Updike has said, "I don't think basically that such parallels should be obvious. I think books should have secrets, like people do. I think they should be there as a bonus for the sensitive reader . . . as a kind of subliminal quavering."[27] Symbolism operates much the same way in Updike's work, and espcially in the "Rabbit" novels. It is not difficult to picture him laboring over charts and outlines while composing, the way Joseph Heller did while writing *Catch-22,* in order to provide that "bonus." Just as Heller carefully built his complicated novel around the idea of military bureaucracy, in *Rabbit Redux* Updike chose the Apollo moonshot—and the moon, generally—as his central metaphor. The result is no less unified than in Heller's novel, and no less accessible to "the sensitive reader." All of *Rabbit Redux's* many subthemes and verbal intricacies are contained within, or are reflected by, this one integrating symbol, which functions throughout as a point of reference, lending the book a wholeness and cohesiveness by uniting all of the seemingly disparate elements.

Updike does not intend, however, for the moon to convey any *single* meaning; in *Rabbit Redux* the moon functions as both a positive and a negative image, and finally as a metaphor for tentativeness, duality, irresolution, and qualification. Although all of Updike's works convey a strong sense of reservation, *Rabbit Redux* is the fullest articulation of it. On the one hand, the moon serves a positive function, as the Apollo moonshot embodies the idea of human ingenuity and aspiration. Certainly, the image of the thrusting rocket suggests an upward orientation, and can also be seen as a phallic symbol, connoting regeneration, life, and futurity. But the moon has, of course, both its light and its dark sides, and in

Rabbit Redux the moon's constant presence is often a reminder
of the dark aspects of contemporary America. Although the
moonshot represents a major technological breakthrough,
technology is usually suspect in Updike's work, and in *Rabbit
Redux* the reader is constantly reminded that the astronauts'
success has little or no bearing on the often distressing realities encountered in everyday life. Indeed, Updike continually creates an almost humorous sense of disparity between the
doings of the astronauts and those of earthbound characters.
In the opening barroom scene, for example, the murmuring
drinkers watch the televised lift-off, but *they* "have not been
lifted, they are left here" (p. 7). At one point, Rabbit admonishes Jill, the "moonchild" (p. 202), that the moon "is cold
. . . . Cold and ugly" (p. 170), and his estimate of the Apollo
mission is equally negative: "these guys see exactly where
they're aiming and it's a big round nothing" (p. 22). This
same sense of impatience with the supposed glories of lunar
exploration emerges also in Updike's poem of the same period, "Seven New Ways of Looking at the Moon," which
opens as follows:

> Man, am I sick
>   of the moon.
> We've turned it into one big
>   television screen,
> one more littered campsite,
> one more high school yearbook
>   signed, "Lots of luck,
>   Richard Nixon."[28]

But it would be a mistake to interpret Harry's "summer of
the moon" (p. 201) as simply a peevish authorial denigration
of the space program, for Harry achieves through his experiences a very real (if tenuous) resurrection from the deadening

torpor into which he has fallen during the ten years since the events of *Rabbit, Run*. If he is first pictured in *Rabbit Redux* as simply another disgruntled patron of the Phoenix Bar, by the novel's conclusion he has achieved the rebirth that his mother advised him to pray for (p. 198), rising from his own ashes like the mythical Phoenix. Although his house has been torched by irate neighbors angered by Harry's involvement with Skeeter and Jill, the fire serves almost as a rite of purification for Harry. He acquires a fuller understanding of his own life, and appears to be finally on the path to self-realization. Updike seems to be suggesting that truth can be found only in the congruence of opposites, and that reality must be confronted as it is, with all its basic anomalies. The moon, both dark and light, and hot and cold, associated in myth with good and evil, and thought of as embodying both male and female principles, serves as an exceptionally effective metaphor for such an idea, literally embodying it.

Updike draws upon all of these aspects of the moon's associative potential, as he explores his themes of black-white relations, sexual ambiguity, and moral conflict. Each of the book's four chapters is prefaced by fragments of the actual recorded conversations between Russian cosmonauts or American astronauts, and the novel's final pages, in which Harry achieves a sort of uneasy resolution in his new recognition of life's complexity, are filled with references to the moonshot. As Harry and his wife Janice are reunited, they are likened to space vehicles, "slowly revolving, afraid of jarring one another away" (p. 396). Harry feels as if he and Janice "are . . . adjusting in space, slowly twirling. . . . In a space of silence . . . he feels them drift along sideways deeper into being married" as they "joggle in space" (p. 405). Nothing is simple in this novel, and Updike's message seems to be that no clearcut vision of good and evil as distinct conceptions is possible. Harry remarks that "confusion is just a local view of things working out in general" (p. 405), and the framing device of the moon metaphor reinforces the novel's celebration of ambiguity, tentativeness, and contradiction.

This ongoing interplay of positive and negative connotation is most dramatically embodied in Updike's handling of the black characters in the novel. Throughout, Harry is both attracted and repelled by the various blacks he encounters, and this duality of response is most strongly elicited by Skeeter. On the one hand, the black characters seem to represent to Harry the vital life force that he (like the white population at large) has lost, and the frigid ambiance of the Phoenix Bar contrasts sharply with the sensuous, murky environment of the all-black Jimbo's Lounge, where Babe the pianist plays songs—"all the good old ones" (p. 123)—that conjure up the past. Babe's singing "frightens Rabbit with its enormous black maw of truth yet makes him overjoyed that he is here; he brims with joy, to be here with these black others, he wants to shout love" (p. 125). But Skeeter, of course, remains a satanic figure. Although he constitutes a source of revivification and enlightenment for Harry, not only by reawakening the spontaneous, visceral components of Harry's personality, but also by instructing Harry in some of the more sordid realities of American history, he is ultimately a bearer of destruction and death. This contrast is typical of the novel's whole method.

Repeatedly, the idea of contrariety is stressed, frequently through linking of hot and cold, darkness and paleness (and specifically, black and white). At one point Harry's supper of chicken livers has "burned edges and icy centers" (p. 275). Viewing photographs of his charred house, Harry notes that it is only "half-burned" and that the burned half contrasts sharply with the unburned half (p. 351). A television skit that Harry watches depicts comedians Sammy Davis, Jr., and Arte Johnson confronting each other in the same role; the black actor and the white "sit side by side and stare at each other. They are like one man looking into a crazy mirror" (p. 247). Although on one level such details can be considered simply as literal renderings of commonplace actualities, their sheer numbers suggest that they also function on the symbolic plane, with the moon—in all of its ambiguity—serving always as backdrop.

Certainly *Rabbit Redux* is the most broadranging and multifaceted of Updike's novels, and is also his most highly symbolic work. Indeed, despite the book's historical accuracy and plethora of realistic detail, its dominant impression is not so much that of documentary but of poetic fictionalization; surely this is partially the result of Updike's masterly use of symbolism throughout. "*Rabbit Redux* is not grounded in history and reinforced by fictive imagery; it is based on the imagery and is reinforced by history."[29] The same might be said of Updike's fiction generally, and of Roth's as well. Both writers invest the commonplace with an almost mythic dimension through the transmuting magic of literary craft.

7

Other Modes: Roth and Updike as Experimental Writers

B OTH ROTH AND UPDIKE can be most accurately described as social realists. They generally prefer the literal rendering of relatively commonplace actualities and avoid highly esoteric flights in the manner of, say, John Hawkes. Each has produced, however, a certain number of what might be called "experimental" fictions. Generally sportive and quirky, these idiosyncratic departures nevertheless tend in most cases to reflect the writers' ongoing concerns.

Roth's experimental ventures, for example, address such issues as Jewish-American identity, the relationship between artifice and truth (especially in the area of "official" versions of truth), and personal responsibility and guilt. Updike has also utilized experimental effects to pursue certain of his dominant interests: the unique quality of American small-town life, the tentative gropings of adolescence, and the undercurrent of sensuality that so largely motivates his characters' behavior. The principal difference between the two writers' use of experimental approaches is one of proportion;

Roth has indulged the experimental impulse more often and to a greater extent than Updike, a fact that takes on added significance in view of Roth's smaller corpus. Whereas Updike has ventured into experimentalism in an occasional, intermittent sort of way, Roth for an extended period in his career embraced experimentalism exclusively, producing a whole series of unconventional works.

Portnoy's Complaint signaled a departure from Roth's accustomed mode of Jamesian realism, and the beginning of a five year period of literary experimentation that was to produce two more novels, two short stories, and three political sketches: *The Breast* and *The Great American Novel*; "On the Air" and " . . . Looking at Kafka"; and *Our Gang*, "A Modest Proposal," and "The President Addresses the Nation." These works may be aptly—if punningly—described as Roth's "jeu-ish American" fictions, because of their highly irregular, playful nature. As John N. McDaniel has pointed out, they reveal a movement in Roth's fiction toward the vernacular and the satirical, while emphasizing "the most prominent features of Roth's sensibility: his increasing pessimism over the possibilities for selfhood, his attention to the social landscape . . . and his continuing concern with moral and psychological crises experienced in and perpetuated by American . . . life."[1] *Portnoy's Complaint* and the fictions that followed it constitute Roth's literary application of the principle outlined in his "Writing American Fiction" essay, the notion that in contemporary America, truth is indeed "stranger than fiction," dwarfing the novelist's capacity for invention. It is not surprising, therefore, that in attempting to come to terms with this situation, Roth turned in his post-*Portnoy* period to creating fictions so bizarre as to outstrip the putative excesses of the American scene, and on their own outlandish terms.

The long story "On the Air" is a particularly good example of this development. Although seriously weakened—indeed, rendered finally chaotic—by a lack of direction and resolution, the story is noteworthy for its extremely high level of inventiveness and antic comedy. Many of the bizarre episodes, hilarious one-liners, and comic routines that distinguish this story reveal even better than *Portnoy's Complaint* the remarkable range and flexibility of its author's comic gift. Further, "On the Air" typifies Roth's new mode of irreverence, especially as applied to specifically ethnic material.

On the literal level, the story chronicles the efforts of Milton Lippman, a small-time Jewish talent scout, to organize an "Answer Man" type of radio show that will challenge the currently popular goyische version (the story is set in the 1940s) by featuring none other than Albert Einstein, thus (in Lippman's words) "showing those goyim what smart really means."[2] But Lippman is a pathetic figure, a small-minded, paranoic, self-deluding crackpot. Nevertheless, many of his observations concerning the vacuity and cheapness of the American popular culture of his day (and, by implication, of our own) are grounded in truth. The suggestion is that the vulgar stereotypes and inane oversimplifications that characterize popular thought reduce everyone, Jews and Gentiles alike, to the level at which only grotesque distortions are possible.

In addition, Roth seems to imply that in a sense, unreality is the norm in a world gone mad. This is the connotation of Lippman's philosophy: "what you could imagine could also be so . . . everyplace you looked today . . . there was entertainment material galore . . . . what if the world is some kind of—of show. . . . What if we are all only talent assembled by The Great Talent Scout Up Above. The Great Show of Life! Starring Everybody! Suppose entertainment is the

Purpose of Life!" (pp. 16, 19, 20) Such implications are reinforced by the story's heavily surrealistic manner, an element
of its conception which, along with its scatological coloration,
has caused it to be compared to the work of William S. Burroughs and Hubert Selby.[3] Unfortunately, the story's skillful
blend of realism and surrealism, and of uproarious comedy
and serious insinuation, dissolves into sheer tomfoolery in
the last two sections of the piece. The reader is left feeling
tricked and unsatisfied. Roth is aware of the inconclusive nature of this interesting but finally erratic work; he has said
that "I couldn't go further with it because the dreadful comic
fantasies of persecution and humiliation depicted there were,
to my mind, decidedly 'Jewish.' "[4]

Perhaps this is why Roth switched, in his next three productions, to material that maintained the satirically comic
emphasis of *Portnoy's Complaint* and "On the Air," but es-
chewed their "decidedly 'Jewish' " emphasis. Unfortunately,
however, Roth was unable, at least in *Our Gang* and *The
Breast,* to maintain a consistently high level of creativity, and
only *The Great American Novel* warrants serious consideration.
Our Gang, Roth's scathing but humorous satire on Richard
Nixon, is an interesting exercise in the manipulation of language (and in that sense shares certain affinities with Roth's
"midwestern" novel, *When She Was Good*), but is flawed by a
number of serious weaknesses. Probably the tenor of the
times, more than anything else, accounts for the unwarrant-
ed enthusiasm of several early reviews.[5] *Our Gang* could have
served as an entertaining magazine piece, rather along the
lines of Roth's other short political satires, "Positive Thinking on Pennsylvania Avenue," "A Modest Proposal," and
"The President Addresses the Nation," but as a full-length
work, the book is negligible. As Roth himself has observed,
"political satire isn't writing that lasts. Though satire, by and

large, deals with enduring social and political problems, its comic appeal lies in the use made of the situation of the moment."[6] *Our Gang* remains a political satire rather than a true novel, and as such it represents little more than a playfully negligible digression in any total assessment of Roth's career.

In *The Breast,* Roth turned once again to narrative fiction. Nevertheless, this novel—really a long story, despite its publication as a (slim, large-print) book—resembles *Our Gang* in that it too is predicated on a gimmick. David Alan Kepesh (the same Kepesh who is the protagonist of the later *The Professor of Desire,* the events of which actually predate those of *The Breast*) is an intelligent young Jewish academic who suffers an amazing "endocrinopathic catastrophe . . . a hermaphroditic explosion of chromosomes"[7] that transforms him into a huge female breast. That Kepesh's situation is bizarre is not, however, what renders the work ultimately indefensible. Highly successful stories have been built on similar conceits, and Kepesh himself remarks that his experience is reminiscent of Gogol's "The Nose" and Kafka's "The Metamorphosis," both of which he has taught as a professor of comparative literature at SUNY-Stonybrook. Rather, the problem here is one of tone; there is a self-defeating sense of unresolved vacillation between comic allegory and somber tragedy. The reader is inclined to ask, in paraphrase of the Marx Brothers, "Why a breast?" The very ludicrousness of Kepesh's metamorphosis undercuts the book's potentially tragic dimension. It is neither Gogol nor Kafka who is really evoked, but Woody Allen.

The Great American Novel, Roth's next book, is perhaps his quirkiest full-length work, and differs markedly in many important respects from almost everything else he has written. It is surely the most successful of Roth's novels published during this period of freewheeling literary experimentation.

Further, Roth's own comments on the book—contained in a playfully revealing (self-conducted) "interview" first published in the *Partisan Review* and entitled "On *The Great American Novel*"—constitute the most enlightening single document concerning this period of Roth's career. In it he grants that *The Great American Novel* "follows its own comic logic—if one can speak of the 'logic' of farce, burlesque, and slapstick—rather than the logic of political satire or a personal monologue"; he then asserts that the book's comedy "exists for the sake of no higher value than comedy itself; the redeeming value is not social or cultural reform, or moral instruction, but *comic inventiveness*. Destructive, or lawless, playfulness—and for the fun of it."[8]

Surely, much of Roth's work since *Portnoy's Complaint* has drawn on the comic tradition of irreverent demythologization. Roth claims that the events of the 1960s, the "demythologizing decade," along with increased self-confidence, had a liberating effect on him: "This . . . expressed itself . . . in a greater willingness to be deliberately, programmatically perverse—subversive not merely of the 'serious' values of official literary culture . . . but . . . of my own considerable investment . . . in seriousness. . . . I set myself the goal of becoming the writer some Jewish critics had been telling me I was all along: irresponsible, conscienceless, *unserious*. Ah, if only they knew what that entailed! And the personal triumph that such an achievement would represent."[9] Obviously, in terming his new method "irresponsible, conscienceless, *unserious*," Roth is referring to the surfaces of his work, rather than to its underlying concerns. As Wilfred Sheed has perceptively stated, Roth has abandoned "the sonorous tones of a major writer. An anxious wise guy, a quintessential punk with a fast, shallow mind is more like it. And don't think it doesn't take craft and hard work and real literary intelligence

. . . to achieve that effect."[10] Roth's own comments reinforce Sheed's observations: "One of my continuing problems as a writer has been to find the means to be true to these seemingly inimical realms of experience that I am strongly attached to by temperament and training—the aggressive, the crude, and the obscene, at one extreme, and something a good deal more subtle and, in every sense, refined, at the other."[11]

The questions with which Roth continues to deal partake of his penchant for the subtle, the refined, and the serious, while the satirical, scatological approach that he adopted during his experimental period satisfied his need to indulge his more "questionable" leanings. Having thus unburdened himself, Roth was then able to concentrate more fully on perfecting his artistic skills, using the experimental fictions as, in effect, a form of literary exploration. Further, and perhaps more importantly, these works served also as a vehicle for certain ideas that Roth (apparently) felt morally compelled to pursue, in a public way, at that point in his career. Flawed in their various ways, however, the "jeu-ish American" fictions are significant not so much in themselves but in terms of Roth's development as an artist, and in terms of the level of proficiency that they enabled him finally to attain in the "Salad Days" section of *My Life as a Man,* in the highly polished *The Professor of Desire,* and in the "Zuckerman" novels.

The achievement represented by these recent fictions was presaged, however, by "'I Always Wanted You to Admire My Fasting'; or, Looking at Kafka." Though largely neglected by the critics, ". . . Looking at Kafka" is the most intrinsically accomplished of Roth's experimental writings. The last of Roth's experiments, it far surpasses his other free-wheeling post-Portnoy productions.

For want of a more convenient label, I shall be referring to this compact and almost perfectly balanced work as a short

story. Really it is a highly original blend of biographical literary criticism and fictionalized autobiography. Juxtaposing
two sections of nearly equal length, Roth deals first with the
historical Kafka, the Kafka of actuality, providing a sensitive
and perceptive rendering of the known details of the artist's
last years. He then goes on to construct a fascinating fiction
based on "what might have been" had Kafka not died in
1924, but had lived to emigrate to the United States before
the holocaust. That such an idea should have occurred to
Roth, and at that particular point in his career, is not surprising, for he had for several years been fascinated by Kafka.
Roth once said that he had originally been "sensitized to Kafka's tales of spiritual disorientation and obstructed ener-
gies"[12] by his own bouts with frustration. Indeed, Kafka is
mentioned—or invoked—in a number of Roth's works. It is
almost as if, having finally broken through to a more defined
sense of personal and artistic selfhood, Roth was in effect
pausing to pay homage to the artist who, he says, "furnished
me with any number of clues as to how to give imaginative
expression to preoccupations of my own."[13]

Much in the fashion of Kurt Vonnegut in the first chapter
of *Slaughterhouse-Five,* Roth inserts himself directly into the
work, bypassing the options of using a persona or an anony-
mous, omniscient narrator. Thus he deftly achieves a sense
both of verisimilitude and of felt immediacy in the very first
sentence: "I am looking, as I write of Kafka, at the photo tak-
en of him at the age of forty."[14] After expounding on the details of the photo, Roth then introduces the whimsical suggestion that will provide the controlling idea for the whole
undertaking: the intriguing thought that, given the caprices
of fortune, Kafka might just as well have lived, and, perhaps
with the help of Max Brod or Thomas Mann, have (like
Joseph K. of *Amerika*) fled to this country. And, in one long

and deliberately serpentine—but exquisitely controlled—
sentence, he gracefully effects (in the last verb, "keeps") a
completely subtle transition from the immediate present of
the moment of composition to the "past present" of the imagined moment being described:

The Jewish refugee arriving in America in 1938 would not then
have been Mann's "religious humorist" but a frail and bookish
fifty-five-year-old bachelor, formerly a lawyer for a government insurance firm in Prague, retired on a pension in Berlin at the time of
Hitler's rise to power—an author, yes, but of a few eccentric stories, mostly about animals, stories no one in America had ever
heard of and only a handful in Europe had read; a homeless K., but
without K.'s willfulness and purpose, a homeless Karl, but without
Karl's youthful spirit and resilience; just a Jew lucky enough to
have escaped with his life, in his possession a suitcase containing
some clothes, some family photos, some Prague mementos, and the
manuscripts, still unpublished and in pieces, of *Amerika, The Trial,
The Castle,* and (stranger things happen) three more fragmented
novels, no less remarkable than the bizarre masterworks that he
keeps to himself out of oedipal timidity, perfectionist madness, and
insatiable longings for solitude and spiritual purity. (pp. 248–49)

Accordingly, the rest of section 1 is couched in the present
tense, and the tone of passages such as the above brings the
reader almost into Kafka's own thoughts.

The second section, the fictionalized account of Roth's
apocryphal childhood acquaintance with "my Hebrew-
school teacher, Dr. Kafka" (p. 258), is also written in the
present tense, and flows naturally out of the narrative ambience of the first. Although Kafka's death has already been re-
ported, section 2 seems nonetheless plausible, for having
been lulled into a mood of credulous acceptance by the almost conversational tone of what has gone before—of events
that are, after all, verifiably true—we tend not to resist the
similar tone of section 2. Indeed, having become in a sense

personally involved in Kafka's fate, we almost welcome the alternative version that is now offered and which seems to constitute, in effect, a reprieve.

In detailing the imaginary relationship between Kafka and the Roth family, Roth manipulates the language of the narrative in a highly calculating, deliberate way, varying the syntax and the rhythms of his prose to effectively evoke the very personalities of his subjects. In the following paragraphs, for example, Roth uses direct quotation sparingly, but calls upon *erlebte Rede,* an artful form of narrational paraphrase that in each case not only summarizes action but captures and conveys the personality and conversational mannerisms of the character upon whom the passage is focused. He creates thereby a chorus of voices: the I-narrator, the father (who is both impersonated by the narrator, and also quoted directly), the mother, and Kafka himself:

Does my father do a job on Kafka! Does he make a sales pitch for familial bliss! What it means to a man to have two fine boys and a wonderful wife! Can Dr. Kafka imagine what it's like? The thrill? The satisfaction? The pride? He tells our visitor of the network of relatives on his mother's side that are joined in a "family association" of over two hundred people located in seven states, including the state of Washington! Yes, relatives even in the Far West: here are their photographs, Dr. Kafka; this is a beautiful book we published entirely on our own for five dollars a copy, pictures of every member of the family, including infants, and a family history by "Uncle" Lichtblau, the eighty-five-year-old patriarch of the clan. This is our family newsletter, which is published twice a year and distributed nationwide to all the relatives. This, in the frame, is the menu from the banquet of the family association, held last year in a ballroom of the "Y" in Newark, in honor of my father's mother on her seventy-fifth birthday. My mother, Dr. Kafka learns, has served *six consecutive years* as the secretary-treasurer of the family association. My father has served a two-year term as president, as have each of his three brothers. We now have fourteen boys in the family in uniform. Philip writes a letter on V-mail stationery to five of his cousins in the army every single month. "Religiously," my mother puts in, smoothing my hair. "I firmly believe," says my father, "that the family is the cornerstone of everything." (pp. 261–62)

Dr. Kafka, who has listened with close attention to my father's spiel, handling the various documents that have been passed to him with great delicacy and poring over them with a kind of rapt absorption that reminds me of myself over the watermarks of my stamps, now for the first time expresses himself on the subject of family; softly he says, "I agree," and inspects again the pages of our family book. "Alone," says my father, in conclusion, "alone, Dr. Kafka, is a stone." Dr. Kafka, setting the book gently down upon my mother's gleaming coffee table, allows with a nod that that is so. (p. 262)

In the first paragraph, the rapid pace of the language creates a staccato, incremental effect. The opening sentences— short, successive bursts of exclamation and interrogation— are followed by several longer sentences composed of similarly cumulative segments. These are followed in turn by several more short, emphatic citations of various supposed joys of family life. Roth thus makes palpable the high-pressure, hard-sell approach that his ebullient, "undiscourageable" (p. 260) father (who was in fact an insurance salesman) brings to bear in his attempt to interest Kafka in the forty-year-old spinster, Aunt Rhoda. The "sales pitch" then concludes with the father's dogmatic summary statement, "the family is the cornerstone of everything."

In the paragraph that describes Kafka's reception of these well-intentioned but facile platitudes, the language and sentence structure undergo a radical but entirely appropriate shift. The opening sentence is rather long, and conveys a sense of sober, considered moderation; the verbs (listened, handling, poring, expresses, inspects) and noun phrases (close attention, great delicacy, rapt absorption) serve to suggest Kafka's "precise . . . professorial manner" (p. 258), his "remote and melancholy foreignness" (p. 258), his "Old World ways" (p. 261). The dichotomy between Kafka and the elder Roth is then underscored once again, as another of the matchmaker's categorical (and unwittingly insulting) aphorisms—"Alone . . . is a stone"—is juxtaposed with another lengthy, deliberate sentence that again reflects, through its tone, pace, and structure, the contrastingly polite, formal tentativeness of the beleagured Kafka.

This authorial precision with regard to language is but one aspect of the highly controlled nature of ". . . Looking at Kafka." The piece contains nothing gratuitous; every detail functions organically to establish the precise mood and tone that Roth desires. Accordingly, even the many humorous touches are introduced in a manner that reveals great selectivity and discretion on Roth's part. If Roth exhibited in works such as "On the Air," *Our Gang,* and *The Breast* a tendency to overindulge the comic impulse, ". . . Looking at Kafka" is an example of admirable restraint in that area. Perhaps the difference between the comic elements in ". . . Looking at Kafka" and those of Roth's earlier works is, however, as much one of kind as of degree.

Unlike the humor of *Portnoy's Complaint,* "On the Air," *Our Gang,* et al., the comic elements in ". . . Looking at Kafka" are by their nature rather low-key. There is no slapstick here, no farce, no burlesque, and nothing that could be considered ribald. Rather, in this work a comedic undertone is achieved through subtle devices such as irony and understatement, and through the adult author's wryly amused, retrospective handling of his own childhood perceptions. We learn, for example, that although he is "the most studious member" of the beginners' Hebrew class (p. 259), the young Roth also has a mischievous side that enables him to entertain his classmates—especially the "demonic Schlossman" and the "babyish Ratner" (p. 259)—with such pranks as naming the gloomy Hebrew teacher "Kishka." But when the class enthusiastically adopts this name, Roth experiences feelings of guilt that lead him to embrace "redemptive fantasies of heroism" (p. 259) such as those that he frequently entertains "about the 'Jews in Europe'" (p. 259). Roth then learns the "shocking" news that Kafka resides in a rented room. Remorseful, the student invites his teacher home to dinner, and the humorous liaison between Kafka and the author's family results. Roth's father immediately attempts to "marry off" Aunt Rhoda, launching into the amusing monologue cited above. He sets about his task with even greater than usual energy, for he knows that "Aunt Rhoda is 40 years old—it is not exactly a shipment of brand-new goods that he is trying to move" (p. 264).

Much comedy ensues as the fretful, prudish Rhoda falls in love with the refugee Dr. Kafka, who begins to refer to her in his diary as "R." When Kafka "calls and takes . . . Aunt Rhoda to a movie," young Roth is "astonished, both that he calls and that she goes; it seems there is more desperation in life than I have come across yet in my fish tank" (p. 264). It turns out that "ever since he arrived on these shores Dr. Kafka has wanted to see the famous boardwalk and the horse that dives from the high board" (p. 267)—material that Roth had played for laughs already in "On the Air"—so Kafka and Aunt Rhoda spend a weekend in Atlantic City. However, some sort of misunderstanding (evidently of a sexual nature) occurs, and the romance is ended. Years later, while away at college, Roth receives from his mother a newspaper clipping from which he learns that Kafka has died at the age of 70 in the Deborah Heart and Lung Center in Browns Mills, New Jersey. "Remember poor Kafka," the mother writes, "Aunt Rhoda's beau?" (p. 269).

Clearly, there is abundant humor in all of this, but it is humor of a thoughtful, ruminative kind, and is far-removed from the wild ribaldry of Roth's earlier experimental fictions. This is consistent with the overall intentions of the work. Although decidedly unconventional in form, ". . . Looking at Kafka" is in all respects a pensive, speculative piece of literature, one that in its very conception differs sharply from *Portnoy's Complaint* (which is "serious" in its substance alone) and the other works discussed in this chapter. It constitutes a remarkably skillful blending of Roth's earlier, Jamesian moralism and his later commitment to experimental technique.

There is, moreover, an immediately obvious thematic difference between this work and virtually everything else that preceded it: in ". . . Looking at Kafka" Roth completely abandons the oracular and doctrinaire. For once, he has, so to speak, no *personal* axe to grind. Of course, the work has a thesis, presented in the concluding paragraph: "It simply is not in the cards for Kafka ever to become *the* Kafka—why, that would be stranger even than a man turning into an insect. No one would believe it, Kafka least of all" (p. 270). Roth suggests that, ironically, the truth of Kafka's life was indeed far stranger, far more remarkable, than even a fictive reworking of it could hope to be. He insinuates that Kafka, like the hunger artist, was an individual driven by strange, almost preternatural compulsions that were at once his downfall and the prerequisite conditions of his greatness. But such a proposition is hardly "new"; Roth seeks not to establish an argument, but to construct a humbly reverential expression of homage. In ". . . Looking at Kafka" there is no aggressive assertion of any heterodox position, and none of the belligerance or stridency that so often appears in Roth's other experimental writings.

This is especially evident in Roth's handling of the ethnic ingredients of his narrative. Although ". . . Looking at Kafka" is certainly, with regard to its characters, its setting, and its subject, a very "Jewish" work, Roth's preoccupation with Jewishness *per se* is largely absent. After all but abandoning Jewish material in *Our Gang, The Breast,* and *The Great American Novel,* he seems to have returned to it in ". . . Looking at Kafka" with a decidedly mellowed perspective. The Jewish features of this work are not, as in *Goodbye, Columbus, Portnoy's Complaint,* or "On the Air," *the* issue, but exist simply as natural components of the piece, totally in concert with its larger thematic purposes.

It would seem that with ". . . Looking at Kafka" Roth finally reached the point at which he no longer found it necessary either to criticize or celebrate his ethnic heritage. Having apparently realized that the contemporary Jewish-American cultural situation is his one truly natural artistic milieu, and that this need not result in counterproductive ethnic self-denigration, Roth produced in ". . . Looking at Kafka" what is surely one of his most impressive short works. The most skillfully controlled of his "jeu-ish" fictions and the most balanced and considered of his Jewish fictions, ". . . Looking at Kafka" occupies a position of significance in Roth's corpus, even if his other experimental works do not. In any event, however, Roth's period of experimentation must be seen as a necessary, integral, clearly defined phase of his artistic development.

This is not true in the case of John Updike, for whom experimentalism has represented simply an occasional light-hearted digression, or—in *The Centaur,* especially—a means of endowing an otherwise conventional work with an additional artistic dimension. Nevertheless, since the earliest stages of his career Updike has been willing to take risks that can be seen as basically experimental. Usually his readiness to gamble has paid off. Even in *The Poorhouse Fair,* for example, his choice of protagonist and setting—in fact, the whole conception of the book—is highly unusual, especially for a first novel. Although the actual method of the book reflects Updike's characteristic preference for straightforward realism, he opted here for a futuristic, anti-utopian reference frame that is by definition somewhat experimental, thereby establishing himself as an innovative and artistically uninhibited novelist even in his first fictional venture.

This originality has continued to distinguish Updike's work as he has periodically indulged the experimental impulse, but almost always in a selective and restrained fashion. Unlike Roth, Updike can be said to have utilized unconventional techniques simply to augment his more traditional skills, and at no point in his career has he yielded totally to the temptation of the experimental. Such effects operate in Updike's work to create an impression of literary counterpoint to the predominant realism of his novels and stories. Only in *A Month of Sundays* and the clearly unrepresentative "Other Modes" section of *Museums and Women*—in which he toys with a variety of avant-garde formulations in the manner of Donald Barthelme and other recent practitioners of highly innovative fiction—does he depart at length from conventional technique. Significantly, *A Month of Sundays* is one of Updike's least satisfying novels, and the "Other Modes" sketches constitute barely ten percent of his published short works to date. Usually, the experimental features of Updike's fiction function unobtrusively, as in *Bech: A Book, Rabbit Redux,* and certain shorter works.

In "The Music School," for example, Updike adopts a
rather experimental approach, utilizing an "orchestration of
images replacing a dominant narrative line."[15] The reader is
aware that the narrator is shifting, seemingly at random,
from thought to thought, from topic to topic, and yet the
overall effect is not one of dislocation because the narrative
voice itself is quite familiar and provides a plethora of con-
crete details that lend the piece a sense of structural progression, just as in Updike's two long, semi-autobiographical,
semi-experimental excursions that conclude *Pigeon Feathers:*
"The Blessed Man of Boston, My Grandmother's Thimble,
and Fanning Island," and "Packed Dirt, Churchgoing, A
Dying Cat, A Traded Car." Although Updike's method here
is innovative, these stories are far more realistic in texture
than, say, Roth's "On the Air" or *Our Gang,* because the unusual features of these Updike works are more than offset by
their narrators' traditional deliveries. Whereas Roth often
plunges the reader into a fictional world that can be described
only as bizarre and extreme, Updike seeks always to suggest
the surrealistic quality that lurks just beneath the surface of
quite commonplace events and situations, and his method is
accordingly more reserved.

Congruently, the most obviously experimental features of
Bech: A Book actually exist apart from the Bech stories them-
selves. The same sort of "image orchestration" that charac-
terizes "The Music School" appears also in "The Bulgarian
Poetess," and there are experiments with narrative voice in
"Bech Panics" and in "Bech Swings?" Nevertheless, the
book's principal claim to heterodoxy derives from Updike's
whimsically structuring it as if Bech were an actual person.
The artifice is somewhat similar to that employed by Roth in
My Life as a Man. By prefacing the stories with a letter "from"

Bech "to" Updike himself, and by including two appen-
dixes—"corroborating excerpts from the unpublished Russian journal of Henry Bech" (p. 191) and a mock scholarly
"bibliography" of works by and about Bech—Updike obviously departs from strictly conventional practice, yet this
playful indulgence in no way obtrudes upon the text itself.
And even when Updike does introduce an experimental element directly into a text, as in *Rabbit Redux,* where he inserts
passages of "reproduced" rough copy from Harry Angstrom's linotype machine (a device that Updike may have
learned from Dos Passos but which he could also have borrowed from Roth, who in *Portnoy's Complaint* includes Portnoy's imagined headlines), he does so sparingly, without ever
becoming heavy-handed. In short, Updike's dominant mode
is conventional realism, and his use of experimental effects
has usually been restrained, judicious, and discreet.

On occasion, however, Updike has blundered in this area.
The alternative endings of *Marry Me,* for example, even if
they are read as the speculative musings of the protagonist,
add little to an already unsatisfying work. And in *A Month of
Sundays,* the experimental aspects of the novel are of questionable value. The disjointed and highly euphuistic narrative
voice, although it represents a new departure for Updike, is a
problem; protagonist Marshfield's characterization is over-
shadowed by his own voice. Marshfield's impossibly convo-
luted mode of expression is of course a quite deliberate feature of Updike's whole method in *A Month of Sundays,* but it
does become distracting. One is reminded of the similar nar-
ratorial excesses of Roth's *Great American Novel.* Marshfield's
solipsistic exercise in impromptu prose catharsis is gro-
tesquely festooned with labored puns, digressive asides,
veiled allusions, and Freudian slips by the score, often self-

consciously remarked upon or even footnoted, and always couched in extremely bloated language.

Although *A Month of Sundays* is interesting as an articulation of Updike's vision of contemporary Christianity, and although it includes some undeniably thought-provoking material and a number of genuinely first-rate passages, the book is less than the sum of its parts. Too often the novel reads like a poor parody of Nabokov. Significantly, though, another likeness also suggests itself: the similarity between *A Month of Sundays* and *Portnoy's Complaint*. In both books, the protagonists are intelligent, educated, sophisticated, outwardly successful men who are all but undone by their apparent inability to reconcile the seemingly opposed demands of the spirit and the flesh. Masturbators, cocksmen, egoists, and compulsive monologuists, Portnoy and Marshfield alike attempt to resolve their difficulties by confessing them, each in the context of a "therapeutic" situation: Portnoy on his analyst's couch, and Marshfield at the desert retreat for wayward clergymen. Further, both adopt a highly self-conscious tone of wryly comic exorcism, at once self-torturing and ribald. If Roth's performance in *Portnoy's Complaint* has been likened to that of a borscht-belt or vaudeville comic, Updike's in *A Month of Sundays* has been compared to "Pascal blacked-up and crooning the *Pensees* to a soft-shoe shuffle: crucifixion, as scripted by the Marx Brothers."[16] But it is in the light of precisely such a comparison that *A Month of Sundays'* shortcomings are most pronounced.

While Roth is completely at ease with—and remarkably skilled at—broad, burlesque farce and roisterous slapstick, Updike's humor runs more to witty repartee and intellectualized parody, the type of humor that characterizes his light verse. He once confessed that his "first literary idols" included James Thurber and Robert Benchley,[17] and their influence is obvious, especially in such early feuilletons as "Drinking from a Cup Made Cinchy," "Confessions of A Wild Bore," and "What is a Rhyme?" (a satire on T. S. Eliot's literary criticism). But low comedy is not his forte; similarly, Updike's choice of experimentalism as the dominant mode in *A Month of Sundays* reveals that he is far more effective when he adheres to conventional realism or employs experimental effects in a secondary and complementary manner.

The Centaur is of course the best example of Updike's skill in the latter vein. The novel employs a basically conventional plot line and (for the most part) traditional methods of narration and development, but also incorporates an experimental dimension, achieving a tightly orchestrated fusion of the traditional and the unconventional. Specifically, Updike presents the story of George Caldwell, a saintly but beleagured Olinger High School science teacher. It is narrated by Caldwell's son Peter, who constructs, some fifteen years after the fact, a fondly reminiscent account of "a patch of Pennsylvania in 1947" (p. 293). Now "an authentic second-rate abstract expressionist living in an East Twenty-third Street loft" (pp. 102–103), Peter recreates a three-day period of his adolescence, focusing primarily on his father. Clearly, Peter is Updike himself, and George Caldwell is simply the most fully drawn of a long progression of characters (see, for example, "Flight," "Pigeon Feathers," and "Home") modeled on Updike's own schoolteacher father, Wesley Updike. *The Centaur* is, then, another "Olinger story." But aside from its length, what makes *The Centaur* different from the other Olinger works is its experimental aspect.

Upon the story of George Caldwell, Updike superimposes the myth of Chiron, noblest of the centaurs. The narrative veers back and forth between the mythical context and that of Olinger, alternating from section to section and sometimes switching fictive locales even within the same paragraph or sentence. This feature appears centrally in chapter 1, in which Updike establishes the dual nature of the book. Actually, however, the great bulk of the novel is conventionally written, as Peter Caldwell appears as narrator at the beginning of chapter 2 and proceeds along with a traditional, first person participant account, ostensibly told to his sleeping mistress. Of the book's nine chapters, Peter narrates only three. But these constitute more than half of the novel's total length, while strictly myth-oriented chapters amount to only slightly more than twenty pages, with sections of third person narration (which blend the mythical and the realistic, as in chapter 1) accounting for the rest. Because of its highly evocative quality, however, the mythical element remains operative throughout, even when Updike is not actively exploiting it. There is even a glossary at the end, which provides the reader with a key to each character's mythical referent. Old Pop Kramer, Caldwell's father-in-law, is Kronos; Al Hummel, the garageman, is Hephaestus; Zimmerman, the school principal, is Zeus; and so forth.

The critical response to this unusual novel has been quite mixed. Prominent critics such as Arthur Mizener and George Steiner have dismissed *The Centaur* as self-indulgent trivia, as have several critics who are usually very enthusiastic about Updike's work. Charles Thomas Samuels, for example, complains that the mythological overlay is "pretentious and confusing."[18] On the other hand, there are numerous critics who applaud the book's originality. Larry Taylor maintains that *The Centaur* is "Updike's finest work— the novel which would have established him as a 'major' writer, had he written nothing else."[19] As is so often the case, the truth lies somewhere between these extremes of opinion. There are, in fact, points at which the myth-reality parallel becomes somewhat unwieldy and counterproductive. But if not totally successful, the stratagem generally works well, serving several purposes at once.

On the most obvious level, it enables Updike to invest the subject of his father with considerable grandeur without becoming guilty of sentimentalization. The elevation of George Caldwell to mythic stature is implied rather than stated outright, and is therefore easier for the reader to accept. Caldwell remains, though, a perplexing character and an unlikely hero:

He is a genuinely funny person who delights his students by his unpredictability. He is a compulsively charitable person who allows others to take advantage of him. He is an effusively grateful person who feels obliged to recognize the least kindnesses shown to him by others, even by a hotel clerk. He is an embarrassingly soulful person who ignores the social proprieties to engage anyone he meets in serious discussion, minister, homosexual, or drunk. He is an essentially abstracted person who neglects his clothing and material needs, so much so that his doctor accuses him of a lack of respect for his body. Most of these blundering ways are an annoyance and frustration to Peter.[20]

But if Caldwell is on one level merely an endearing eccentric, on another he is a personage of epic proportions, a mythical figure, Chiron. This accords with the ongoing suggestion running throughout that Caldwell is a teacher not only in the sense of having embraced that particular vocational calling, but by nature. He imparts to Peter a highly moral system of values based on self-sacrifice and dedication. Indeed, just as Chiron gave up his immortality for Prometheus, George Caldwell sacrifices himself for Peter's sake and this sacrifice is no less real for being symbolic. Caldwell's "martyrdom" does not involve an actual loss of life but consists of a willing acceptance of life—significantly, a much diminished life. The implication is that the normal round is a form of death-in-life, which we accept for each other's sake.

By conflating two worlds, that of ancient mythology and that of mundane actuality, Updike further develops the idea that contemporary existence is a disappointing proposition. The modern world, it seems, is inhospitable to the epic spirit. Caldwell is rebuffed and ill-handled at every turn, while the less worthy profit at his expense. As Caldwell himself observes, "It's no Golden Age, that's for sure" (p. 17). This is typical of Updike's method in the novel, as he creates ironic contrast between the events of George Caldwell's world and those of classical antiquity. In this, Updike is indebted to Joyce, who also devised in *Ulysses* an ongoing juxtaposition of classical and modern subject matter.

It would be a mistake, though, to attempt a direct, point by point collation of correspondences between events in the novel and "matching" details from mythology. Rather, the book requires a broader, more impressionistic approach and in fact reflects Updike's familiarity with various experimental techniques from the domain of the visual arts. Detweiler suggests that Updike's approach in *The Centaur* is analogous to certain techniques borrowed from modern painting: "The intention and the effect of the double narrative in *The Centaur* are to expand literal reality through distortion—as in Surrealism (with its accompanying psychological expressive modes)—and through the simultaneous projection of many facets of a personality or action, as in Cubism. . . . As in nonliteral painting, one must grasp the *Gestalt* of the total scene in its equally significant multi-meanings and interrelations instead of trying to discover a cryptic key that logically explains the story."[21]

As with *The Poorhouse Fair,* in which the spirit of the work is more significant than its literal accuracy as social prognostication, *The Centaur* achieves its effects through a combination of intensely realized, realistic depiction, and highly disciplined experimental suggestion. Hence it is not only among the most fully developed and totally engrossing of the autobiographical Olinger fictions, but is also the most successful of Updike's several attempts to employ experimental techniques. It clearly illustrates, however, that Updike is at his most effective when experimental innovation serves a basically supplementary purpose, operating as an enrichment of—rather than as an alternative to—conventional realism. In this sense, *The Centaur* has much in common with Roth's ". . . Looking at Kafka," for although the two works are different, both demonstrate that their authors' experimental impulses yield the most fruitful results when they function in the service of these writers' gifts for realistic depiction.

8

Conclusion:
Assessments and Projections

NOVELISTS OF MANNERS, Roth and Updike are among the most productive living American authors and are currently at the height of their parallel careers. Their fiction not only records with striking fidelity the everyday details and concerns of contemporary American life, but deals also with topics and themes of enduring interest, subjects that have preoccupied writers since the birth of the novel. In exploring these areas of shared concern, they have for the most part called upon the novelist's traditional literary methods. Although on occasion both have ventured into the experimental mode—Roth more often, and more daringly—and achieved some success by employing unconventional techniques, their best work is predominantly realistic. In the course of their prolific careers, they have enjoyed both popular and critical acclaim, attracting an enormous general readership and generating an abundance of scholarly commentary.

As critic Martin Amis has said, "Philip Roth's . . . novels arrange themselves in trilogies—or they do if you nudge them."[1] There is the early period of Jamesian moralism that produced *Goodbye, Columbus, Letting Go,* and *When She Was Good.* Then followed Roth's "experimental period," which actually began with *Portnoy's Complaint,* but which (by virtue of the sort of "nudge" to which Amis alludes) can be said to comprise *Our Gang, The Breast,* and *The Great American Novel.* There is the confessional "Trilogy of Desire": *Portnoy's Complaint, My Life as a Man,* and *The Professor of Desire.* And now, of course, there is the "Zuckerman" trilogy: *The Ghost Writer, Zuckerman Unbound,* and *The Anatomy Lesson.* Similarly, despite certain anomalies (such as *The Poorhouse Fair,* the "Bech" books, and *The Coup,* which do not really "fit") Updike's corpus can also be rather neatly subcategorized: the "Olinger" fictions (*The Centaur, Of the Farm,* and certain stories); the "Rabbit" novels (*Rabbit, Run, Rabbit Redux* and *Rabbit Is Rich*); and the "suburbia" fictions (*Couples, A Month of Sundays, Marry Me,* and certain stories—most typically, the "Maples" stories and the *Problems* stories).

Further, both writers have published numerous articles, nonfiction essays, reviews, and the like, which they have collected in miscellanies: Roth's *Reading Myself and Others,* and Updike's *Assorted Prose, Picked-Up Pieces,* and *Hugging the Shore.* While Roth has edited Penguin's "Writers From the Other Europe" series, Updike has been more active in the nonfiction vein than has Roth, contributing regularly to *The New Yorker,* first as a "The Talk of the Town" staff reporter, and more recently as a book reviewer. In addition, Updike has also published four volumes of poetry, a play, and several children's books, thereby qualifying as perhaps the most versatile "man of letters" in America today. Indeed, critic Donald Grenier recently published a book-length study, *The Other John Updike: Poems/Short Stories/Prose/Play* (Ohio Univ. Pr., 1981), which assesses Updike in this context. In any case, though, both Roth and Updike are major literary figures whose work is rather diverse and continues to be read, studied, and discussed, both within and outside of academe.

However, neither writer's career has been problem-free. Despite his heady initial successes, Roth later struggled through some lean years, producing several works that contributed little to his reputation. The subsequent autobiographical excesses of *My Life as a Man* then gave rise to a chorus of "faint praise," exemplified by Michael Wood's damning remark that "the book . . . shows us . . . a very talented writer slightly at odds with his talent."[2] But now that Roth has regained his stride with *The Professor of Desire* and the "Zuckerman" novels, his early promise seems certain to be fully realized. Likewise, Updike has recently survived a creative slump. Within three years (1973–1976) he produced three seriously flawed works: the inert *Buchanan Dying*, the interesting but quirky *A Month of Sundays*, and his least impressive novel, *Marry Me*. Around the same time, he was publishing a series of *New Yorker* stories (later collected in the aptly-named *Problems*) that signalled further difficulties. Although many of these stories are excellent as individual pieces, in the aggregate they seemed to suggest that Updike was entrapping himself in the same sort of obsessively autobiographical chronicling of marital woe that had preoccupied Roth in *My Life as a Man*. But since then, Updike has returned to form, publishing the highly accomplished *Coup*, the excellent *Rabbit Is Rich*, and the generally well-received *Bech Is Back*.

Despite whatever problems have beset these writers, they have nevertheless had a considerable impact on their culture, not only through their own books, but also by their effect on other writers. Like Hemingway and Fitzgerald before them, they have influenced the ways in which we name and envision experience, becoming perhaps the most subtly influential writers of their generation. In the title novella and several of the short stories in *Goodbye, Columbus,* for example, Roth demonstrated a remarkable fidelity to the small details of everyday experience, an acute keenness of observation, and a masterly command of dialogue. *Letting Go,* although somewhat disjointed, is a similarly impressive performance, flawed mainly in the ways that so many good young novelists' first long books tend to be (Baldwin's *Another Country* comes to mind as a convenient point of comparison). *Portnoy's Complaint* is a comic masterpiece, an extraordinary work mined from the American colloquial vein. *The Professor of Desire* and the "Zuckerman" novels are Roth's most mature and most tightly controlled works to date, combining the jaunty flair of his earlier fiction and the disciplined precision of his nonfiction essays.

Likewise, Updike has produced several "major" works: *The Centaur,* in which reality and myth intertwine to create a vivid impression of a place, a time, and a man; the three outstanding "Rabbit" novels, which not only picture the quintessential antihero for our time but also comment trenchantly on the diminished condition of contemporary America; and a wealth of short stories that are admirable examples of that genre, demonstrating Updike's deep understanding of the broad range of human emotion.

The most important critical issue that must be confronted at this point, though, is the question of what Roth and Updike will attempt—and, more significantly, what they will successfully accomplish—in the future, for therein lies the key to their final standing in the American literary pantheon. This question is difficult, however, for both writers are enormously versatile, and are virtually assured of further development. Even when stumbling, they can produce brilliant highlights (such as the long "airport" scene in Updike's

Marry Me, or the "Salad Days" section of Roth's *My Life as a Man*), and when they are at the top of their form they never fail to surprise. Roth has occasionally gone extremely far afield of his accustomed fictive environs. We have seen, for example, how in *When She Was Good* Roth in a sense appropriated Updike's material, writing about the W.A.S.P. mainstream. And in lesser-known short stories such as "Expect the Vandals" and "The Good Girl" he employs similarly uncharacteristic features. Laurie Bowen, the central character in the latter story, was Roth's first female protagonist (and except for Lucy Nelson of *When She Was Good* and Ella Wittig of "The Psychoanalytic Special," his only one). In "Expect the Vandals," the whole fictional situation is utterly unlike anything else Roth has written, as the story concerns two American G.I.'s who are forced into a Robinson Crusoe-like existence when they are stranded on a Pacific atoll after the close of World War II.

Updike too can step entirely out of character when he wishes to do so. This is obvious not only from *The Coup,* which is set in Africa, but also from the highly interesting *Bech: A Book* and *Bech Is Back,* in which he ventured into Roth's domain, portraying a Jewish-American writer. In a way, the "Bech" books can almost be envisioned as a countermove to Roth's earlier *When She Was Good,* and Updike's "Jewish" books have much in common with Roth's "midwestern W.A.S.P." novel. In all of these works, human interaction is impeded and finally thwarted by imposture, role playing, misunderstanding, and, ultimately, by the sheer intransigence and treachery of language itself. Yet Updike's two story collections never drag in the way that *When She Was Good* sometimes does, because the comic elements lend them a buoyancy and flair that mitigate—without negating—the books' more somber aspects. Indeed, this is a standard feature of much bona fide Jewish-American fiction, and Updike seems to have learned this technique. In any case, *Bech: A Book* and *Bech Is Back* are significant in that they represent for Updike a radical change of pace:

He has moved, in *Bech,* out of the rather insular and largely auto-biographical world of his earlier books—a world of cities like Alton and suburbs like Tarbox—and into the greater world beyond it. . . . the people and places in this world seem more . . . objectively seen. . . . they are treated with a new detachment, a distancing. . . . the character of Henry Bech is . . . the first Updike protagonist who is a wholly original creation, in the sense that he shares little or none of the personal history of his author. Rabbit, Piet, and Peter Caldwell were all, in some sense, versions of John Updike; Henry Bech is someone else again.[3]

Bech, as a man of the world—rather in fact, like Roth's recent protagonists Kepesh and Zuckerman—affords his author considerable latitude. The "Bech" collections mark the direction in which Updike's career might most productively move: into new and previously unexplored areas of creative possibility. Of course, Updike has said that there will be another "Rabbit" novel: "I . . . hope to rendezvous with my ex basketball player and fellow pilgrim one more time."[4] But the likelihood is that Updike will continue to discover and explore new territory as well.

Roth is also at an important point in his development. His recent achievements do not alter the fact that a bit more variety of content and approach would be helpful. For Roth to pursue the confessional mode any further—at least in novels—would be counterproductive. Surely Roth knows this, but it remains to be seen how he will go about breaking new ground. Many critics have noted that Roth is at his best in short bursts; *Portnoy's Complaint* is the most obvious example of this (consisting of a succession of rapidfire "skits"), but even Roth's longer, more strictly naturalistic novels are, to varying degrees, composed of numerous interlocking vignettes, stories within the story. *Letting Go* is very much this way, including within its far-flung reaches any number of unforgettable, gemlike little episodes that remain sharply etched in the reader's memory: the "Dr. Lumin" scene, for example, in which Libby Herz seeks professional counseling; the "Corngold-Levy" scenes, which focus on the Herzes' elderly neighbors; Gabe Wallach's several encounters with the maddeningly uncooperative Harry Bigoness; and so on. The same is true of *When She Was Good, My Life as a Man, The Professor of Desire,* and the "Zuckerman" novels. Indeed, Roth's ongoing habit of placing numerous prepublication excerpts in various magazines reinforces this impression.

Moreover, Roth has said that at one point he envisioned a "Spielvogel cycle" of related stories focused on a diverse group of people in analysis[5]—a latter-day *Canterbury Tales* sort of arrangement, perhaps. Sanford Pinsker has said that Roth is planning "a collection of essays 'imagining' *other* writers."[6] All of this suggests at least the possibility that Roth may turn back to short works. Indeed, Melvin Maddocks maintains that Roth "may be more naturally a writer of short stories"[7] than of novels, an idea that is supported somewhat by the fact that Roth has written such a high percentage of excellent stories. Practically half of his published stories are superior: the "Columbus" stories (excepting "You Can't Tell a Man by the Song He Sings"), "The Psychoanalytic Special," "On the Air," ". . . Looking at Kafka," and "Salad Days."

In addition, it is quite likely that Roth may begin publishing serious literary criticism as well as his own fiction, for literary analysis has come to occupy an increasingly central position in his novels. The most recent works particularly are filled with literary allusion, exegesis, and commentary. This tendency, nurtured by his intermittent ventures into university teaching, may well develop into something resembling Updike's penchant for scholarly publication. Finally, however, it is his own fiction that will determine his eventual standing.

Even if Roth and Updike were to write nothing more—and that is grossly unlikely—their place in American literary history would be assured. When the period from 1950–2000 is assessed by future commentators, books such as *Goodbye, Columbus, Portnoy's Complaint, The Professor of Desire,* the "Zuckerman" novels, *The Centaur,* the "Rabbit" novels, and certain of Updike's short story collections will not be forgotten. Roth and Updike are among our most important writers, having captured with considerable expertise the spirit and the spiritlessness of the times. George Steiner's comment on Updike is equally applicable to both writers; he describes Updike's fiction as "penetrative into the fabric of American discourse and gesture to a degree that future historians and sociologists will exult in."[8]

Notes

Chapter 1   Roth and Updike

1. Philip Roth, "Writing American Fiction," in *Reading Myself and Others* (New York: Farrar, 1974), 120.
2. Charles Thomas Samuels, *John Updike,* University of Minnesota Pamphlets on American Writers, no. 79 (Minneapolis: Univ. of Minnesota Pr., 1969), 6.
3. Roth, "Writing American Fiction," 121.
4. *Ibid.,* 125.
5. Roth, *Zuckerman Unbound* (New York: Farrar, 1981), 225. Subsequent references to *Zuckerman Unbound* are to this edition; page numbers are parenthesized in the text.

Chapter 2   "Roots"
Ethnic/Cultural Backgrounds in Roth and Updike

1. Sanford Pinsker, *The Comedy that "Hoits": An Essay on the Fiction of Philip Roth,* Literary Frontiers (Columbia: Univ. of Missouri Pr., 1975), dedication page.
2. Roth, "Writing About Jews," in *Reading Myself and Others,* 168.

3. Roth, *Portnoy's Complaint* (New York: Random, 1969), frontispiece. Subsequent references to *Portnoy's Complaint* are to this edition; page numbers are parenthesized in the text.

4. Roth, "How Did You Come to Write That Book, Anyway?" in *Reading Myself and Others,* 38–39.

5. *Ibid.,* 35.

6. Irving Howe, *World of Our Fathers* (New York: Harcourt, 1976), 569–70.

7. Roth, "After Eight Books," in *Reading Myself and Others,* 99.

8. *Ibid.,* 111.

9. Sheldon N. Grebstein, *"Portnoy's Complaint* (Philip Roth)," cassette recording (Deland, Fla.: Everett Edwards, 1973).

10. Anatole Broyard, "A Sort of Moby Dick," review of *Portnoy's Complaint, New Republic,* 1 Mar. 1969, 21.

11. Patricia Meyer Spacks, "About Portnoy," *Yale Review* 58, no. 4 (1969):623.

12. Roth, "On *Portnoy's Complaint,"* in *Reading Myself and Others,* 20.

13. Roth, "Writing About Jews," 158.

14. John Updike, "Toward Evening," in *The Same Door* (New York: Knopf, 1972), 63–64.

15. Updike, "The Blessed Man of Boston, My Grandmother's Thimble, and Fanning Island," in *Pigeon Feathers and Other Stories* (New York: Knopf, 1962), 241–42.

16. Tony Tanner, *City of Words: American Fiction 1950–1970* (New York: Harper and Row, 1971), 277.

17. Updike, *Couples* (New York: Knopf, 1968), 52. Subsequent references to *Couples* are to this edition; page numbers are parenthesized in the text.

18. Updike, *Rabbit, Run* (New York: Knopf, 1960), 127. Subsequent references to *Rabbit, Run* are to this edition; page numbers are parenthesized in the text.

19. Updike, *Rabbit Redux* (New York: Knopf, 1971), 210. Subsequent references to *Rabbit Redux* are to this edition; page numbers are parenthesized in the text.

20. Updike, *Rabbit Is Rich* (New York: Knopf, 1981), 3. Subsequent references to *Rabbit Is Rich* are to this edition; page numbers are parenthesized in the text.

21. George J. Searles, "*The Poorhouse Fair*: Updike's Thesis Statement," in *John Updike*, Critical Essays on American Literature, W. R. MacNaughton, ed. (Boston: G. K. Hall, 1982), *passim*.

22. Broyard, "Twenty Eight Stories and Two Novels," review of *The Poorhouse Fair*, *The New York Times Book Review*, 17 Apr. 1977, 12.

23. Roth, "Writing About Jews," 168.

24. Charles Thomas Samuels, "The Art of Fiction XLIII: John Updike," interview, *Paris Review* 12, no. 45 (1968): 89.

25. Kenneth Hamilton, "John Updike: Chronicler of 'The Time of the Death of God,'" *The Christian Century*, 7 June 1967, 747.

Chapter 3   Fathers and Sons
Family Relationships in Roth and Updike

1. Roth, *Goodbye, Columbus* (Boston: Houghton Mifflin, 1959), 19. Subsequent references to *Goodbye, Columbus* are to this edition; page numbers are parenthesized in the text.

2. Stanley Cooperman, "Philip Roth: 'Old Jacob's Eye' With A Squint," *Twentieth Century Literature* 19, no. 4 (1973): 213.

3. Roth, *The Professor of Desire* (New York: Farrar, 1977), 247. Subsequent references to *The Professor of Desire* are to this edition; page numbers are parenthesized in the text.

4. Roth, *Letting Go* (New York: Random, 1962), 5. Subsequent references to *Letting Go* are to this edition; page numbers are parenthesized in the text.

5. Judith Paterson Jones and Guinevera A. Nance, *Philip Roth* (New York: Ungar, 1981), 69 and 71.

6. Roth, "Document Dated July 27, 1969," in *Reading Myself and Others*, 26.

7. Nora Sayre, "Wild Pigs and Others," review of *When She Was Good*, *New Statesman*, 2 June 1967, 770.

8. *Ibid.*, 770.

9. Jones and Nance, 54.

10. Granville Hicks, "A Bad Little Good Girl," review of *When She Was Good*, *Saturday Review*, 17 June 1967, 25–26.

11. Tanner, 274.
12. Samuels, "The Art of Fiction XLIII: John Updike," 117.
13. Updike, "Why Write?" in *Picked-Up Pieces* (New York: Knopf, 1976), 37.
14. Updike, "Flight," in *Pigeon Feathers and Other Stories* (New York: Knopf, 1962), 50 and 51. Subsequent references to "Flight" are to this edition of *Pigeon Feathers;* page numbers are parenthesized in the text.
15. Updike, *The Centaur* (New York: Knopf, 1963), 47. Subsequent references to *The Centaur* are to this edition; page numbers are parenthesized in the text.
16. Updike, *Of the Farm* (New York: Knopf, 1965), 29. Subsequent references to *Of the Farm* are to this edition; page numbers are parenthesized in the text.
17. Samuels, "The Art of Fiction XLIII: John Updike," 92.
18. Samuels, *John Updike,* 22.
19. Eric Rhode, "BBC Interview: John Updike Talks to Eric Rhode About the Shapes and Subjects of his Fiction," interview, *The Listener,* 19 June 1969, 863.
20. Updike, Introduction to the Czech Edition of *Of the Farm,* in *Picked-Up Pieces,* 83.

Chapter 4   Sons and Lovers
Romantic Involvement and Personal Morality in
Roth and Updike

1. Roth, "On *The Breast,*" in *Reading Myself and Others,* 70.
2. Roth, *My Life as a Man* (New York: Holt, 1974), 238. Subsequent references to *My Life as a Man* are to this edition; page numbers are parenthesized in the text.
3. For a perceptive treatment of Roth's and Updike's portrayals of women, see Mary Allen, *The Necessary Blankness: Women in Major American Fiction of the Sixties* (Urbana: Univ. of Illinois Pr., 1976), *passim.*

4. Martin Amis, "No Satisfaction," review of *The Professor of Desire, New Statesman,* 13 Jan. 1978, 50.

5. Saul Bellow, *Seize the Day* (New York: Viking, 1956), 23.

6. Frank Gado, ed., "A Conversation with John Updike," in *First Person: Conversations on Writers and Writing* (Schendectedy, N.Y.: Union College Pr., 1973), 92.

7. Rhode, 866.

8. Samuels, *John Updike,* 37.

9. Gado, 92.

10. Tanner, 15.

11. Richard Wesley Burr, *Puer Aeternus: An Examination of John Updike's* Rabbit, Run (Zurich: Juris Verlag, 1974).

12. David D. Galloway, *The Absurd Hero in American Fiction* (Austin: Univ. of Texas Pr., 1966), 36–37.

13. Jane Howard, "Can a Nice Novelist Finish First?" *Life,* 4 Nov. 1966, 80.

14. Norris W. Yates, "The Doubt and Faith of John Updike," *College English* 26, no. 4 (1965): 474.

15. Samuels, "The Art of Fiction XLIII: John Updike," 100.

16. Clinton S. Burhans, Jr., "Things Falling Apart: Structure and Theme in *Rabbit, Run,*" *Studies in the Novel* 5, no. 3 (1974): 342.

17. *Ibid.,* 350.

18. Larry E. Taylor, *Pastoral and Anti-Pastoral Patterns in John Updike's Fiction,* Crosscurrents/Modern Critiques (Carbondale: Southern Illinois Univ. Pr., 1971), 111.

Chapter 5   Secondary Themes in Roth and Updike
Materialism, Vocation, the Clergy, and Sport

1. Updike, "Shillington," in *Telephone Poles* (New York: Knopf, 1963), 60.

2. Tanner, 288.

3. Gado, 101–102.

4. Roth, "The Book That I'm Writing," symposium interview, *The New York Times Book Review,* 12 June 1983, 12.

5. Howard, 82.

6. Updike, *Bech Is Back* (New York: Knopf, 1982), 27.

7. Updike, *A Month of Sundays* (New York: Knopf, 1975), 210. Subsequent references to *A Month of Sundays* are to this edition; page numbers are parenthesized in the text.

8. Pinsker, 13–14.

9. Updike, "Seven Stanzas at Easter," in *Telephone Poles,* 72.

10. Benjamin DeMott, "Mod Masses, Empty Pews," review of *A Month of Sundays, Saturday Review,* 8 March 1975, 20.

11. Robert William Lewis, "Sport and the Fiction of John Updike and Philip Roth," (Ph.D. diss., Ohio State 1973).

12. Roth, "My Baseball Years," in *Reading Myself and Others,* 180.

13. Joyce B. Markle, *Fighters and Lovers: Theme in the Novels of John Updike* (New York: New York Univ. Pr., 1973), 43.

14. George J. Searles, "'Rabbit, Gun': Linguistic Evidence of Harry Angstrom's Self-Delusion," *Notes on Contemporary Literature* 8, no. 4 (1978): 10–11.

15. "Showboat," *Dictionary of American Slang* (New York: Crowell, 1975), 474.

16. "Gunner," *Webster's Sports Dictionary* (Springfield, Mass.: Merriam, 1976), 196.

17. Peter Prince, "Old Glories," review of *The Great American Novel, New Statesman,* 21 September 1973, 393.

18. According to John N. McDaniel in *The Fiction of Philip Roth* (Haddonfield, N.J.: Haddonfield House, 1974), 161, Word Smith was "modeled after Col. John R. Stingo of the old New York *Evening Enquirer.*"

19. Roth, "On The Great American Novel," in *Reading Myself and Others,* 89–92.

20. Ben Siegel, "The Myths of Summer: Philip Roth's *The Great American Novel,*" *Contemporary Literature* 17, no. 2 (1976): 175–76.

21. Robert J. Higgs and Neil D. Isaacs, eds., *The Sporting Spirit: Athletes in Literature and Life* (New York: Harcourt, 1977), 3.

Chapter 6 Modus Operandi
The Literary Method of Roth and Updike

1. D. Keith Mano, "The Novel As Shrug," review of *My Life As A Man, National Review,* 19 July 1974, 828.
2. Roth, "Second Dialogue in Israel," a symposium, *Congress Bi-Weekly,* 16 Sept. 1963, 39.
3. Cooperman, 207.
4. Robert Detweiler, *Four Spiritual Crises in Mid-Century American Fiction* (Gainesville: Univ. of Florida Pr., 1963), 25.
5. Howe, 586, 594–95.
6. Roth, "Writing American Fiction," 131.
7. Roth, "Writing and the Powers That Be," in *Reading Myself and Others,* 11.
8. Roth, "On *Portnoy's Complaint,*" 15.
9. Spacks, 628, 631.
10. John Podhoretz, "Philip Roth, The Great American Novelist," *The American Spectator,* Sept. 1981, 14. See also: Anatole Broyard, "Listener With a Voice," *The New York Times Book Review,* 22 Feb. 1981, 39; G. W. Ireland, "The Voice of Philip Roth," *Queens Quarterly* 87, no. 2 (1980): 286–92; Judith Yaross Lee, "Flights of Fancy," *Chicago Review* 31, no. 4 (1979/80): 46–52.
11. Robert Detweiler, *John Updike* (New York: Twayne, 1972), 38.
12. Tanner, 276.
13. Roth, *The Anatomy Lesson* (New York: Farrar, 1983), 39.
14. Updike, "The Dogwood Tree: A Boyhood," in *Assorted Prose* (New York: Knopf, 1965), 156.
15. Updike, "Shillington," 60.
16. Updike, "The Dogwood Tree: A Boyhood," 186.
17. Samuels, "The Art of Fiction XLIII: John Updike," 91.
18. Updike, "The Dogwood Tree: A Boyhood," 162.
19. Howard, 76.
20. Pinsker, 10–11.

21. Norman Leer, "Escape and Confrontation in the Short Stories of Philip Roth," *Christian Scholar* 49, no. 2 (1966), 137.
22. McDaniel, 105.
23. Roth, "Writing About Jews," 150.
24. Updike, *Bech: A Book* (New York: Knopf, 1970), 67. Subsequent references to *Bech: A Book* are to this edition; page numbers are parenthesized in the text.
25. Samuels, "The Art of Fiction XLIII: John Updike," 116.
26. Markle, 153.
27. Samuels, "The Art of Fiction XLIII: John Updike," 104.
28. Updike, "Seven New Ways of Looking at the Moon," in *Tossing and Turning: Poems* (New York: Knopf, 1977), 53.
29. Detweiler, *John Updike*, 158.

Chapter 7   Other Modes
Roth and Updike as Experimental Writers

1. McDaniel, 150.
2. Roth, "On the Air," *New American Review*, no. 10 (August 1970): 12. Subsequent page references are parenthesized in the text.
3. McDaniel, 153.
4. Roth, "On *The Great American Novel*," 86.
5. See, for example: Dwight MacDonald, "Our Gang," *The New York Times Book Review*, 7 Nov. 1971, 31; Murray Kempton, "Nixon Wins," *The New York Review of Books*, 27 Jan. 1972, 20–22; and Peter S. Prescott, "Joking in the Square," *Newsweek*, 8 Nov. 1971, 110.
6. Roth, "On *Our Gang*," in *Reading Myself and Others*, 43.
7. Roth, *The Breast* (New York: Holt, 1972), 12. Subsequent references to *The Breast* are to this edition; page numbers are parenthesized in the text.
8. Roth, "On *The Great American Novel*," 76.
9. *Ibid.*, 86–87.
10. Wilfred Sheed, "The Good Word: Howe's Complaint," *The New York Times Book Review*, 6 May 1973, 2.

11. Roth, "On *The Great American Novel,*" 82.

12. Roth, "In Search of Kafka and Other Answers," *The New York Times Book Review,* 15 Feb. 1976, 6.

13. *Ibid.*

14. Roth, "'I Always Wanted You to Admire My Fasting'; or, Looking at Kafka," in *Reading Myself and Others* (New York: Farrar, 1975), 247. Subsequent references to ". . . Looking at Kafka" are to this edition of *Reading Myself and Others;* page numbers are parenthesized in the text.

15. Detweiler, *John Updike,* 152.

16. Rosemary Dinnage, "Lusting for God," review of *A Month of Sundays, Times Literary Supplement,* 4 July 1975, 713.

17. Updike, Foreword, in *Assorted Prose,* p. vii.

18. Samuels, *John Updike,* 15.

19. Taylor, 87.

20. Edward P. Vargo, *Rainstorms and Fire: Ritual in the Novels of John Updike* (Port Washington, N.Y.: Kennikat, 1973), 95–96.

21. Detweiler, *John Updike,* 82, 84.

Chapter 8   Conclusion
Assessments and Projections

1. Amis, 50.

2. Michael Wood, "Hooked," review of *My Life as a Man, The New York Review of Books,* 13 June 1974, 10.

3. L. E. Sissman, "John Updike: Midpoint and After," review of *Bech: A Book, Atlantic,* Aug. 1970, 104.

4. Updike, "Updike on Updike," *The New York Times Book Review,* 9 Sept. 1981, 35.

5. Howard Junker, "Will This Finally Be Philip Roth's Year?" *New York Magazine,* 13 Jan. 1969, 44.

6. Pinsker, 121.

7. Melvin Maddocks, "What Makes Lucy Rant?" review of *When She Was Good, The Christian Science Monitor,* 8 June 1967, 11.

8. George Steiner, "Scarlet Letters," review of *A Month of Sundays, The New Yorker,* 10 Mar. 1975, 116.

Selective Bibliography of Books and Critical Essays

On Philip Roth

Allen, Mary. "Philip Roth: When She Was Good She Was Horrid." *The Necessary Blankness: Women in Major American Fiction of the Sixties.* Urbana: Univ. of Illinois Pr., 1976.

Alter, Robert. "The Education of David Kepesh." *Partisan Review* 46, no. 3 (1979): 478–81.

Clerc, Charles. "Goodbye to All That." In *Seven Contemporary Short Novels,* edited by Charles Clerc and Louis Leiter. Glenview, Ill.: Scott, Foresman, 1969.

Cohen, Sarah Blacher. "Philip Roth's Would-Be Patriarchs and Their Shikses and Shrews." *Studies in American Jewish Literature* 1, no. 1 (1975): 16–22.

Cooperman, Stanley. "Philip Roth: 'Old Jacob's Eye' With a Squint." *Twentieth Century Literature* 19, no. 3 (1973): 203–16.

Cushman, Keith. "Looking at Philip Roth Looking at Kafka." *Modern Jewish Studies Annual IV* (1982); joint issue with *Yiddish* 4, no. 4 (1982): 12–31.

Deer, Irving and Harriet Deer. "Philip Roth and the Crisis in American Fiction." *Minnesota Review* 6, no. 4 (1966): 353–60.

Detweiler, Robert. "Philip Roth and the Test of Dialogic Life." *Four Spiritual Crises in Mid-Century American Fiction.* University of Florida Monographs, no. 14. Gainesville: Univ. of Florida Pr., 1963.

Ditsky, John. "Roth, Updike, and the High Expense of Spirit." *University of Windsor Review* 5, no. 1 (1969): 111–20.

Donaldson, Scott. "Philip Roth: The Meanings of *Letting Go.*" *Contemporary Literature* 11, no. 1 (1970): 21–35.

Field, Leslie. "Philip Roth: Days of Whine and Moses." *Studies in American Jewish Literature* 5, no. 2 (1979); joint issue with *Yiddish* 4, no. 1 (1979): 11–14.

Gordon, Lois G. "'PORTNOY'S COMPLAINT': Coming of Age in Jersey City." *Literature and Psychology* 19, nos. 3 and 4 (1969): 57–60.

Graham, Don. "The Common Ground of *Goodbye, Columbus* and *The Great Gatsby.*" *Forum* 13, no. 3 (1976): 68–71.

Grebstein, Sheldon N. "The Comic Anatomy of *Portnoy's Complaint.*" In *Comic Relief: Humor in Contemporary American Literature,* edited by Sarah Blacher Cohen. Urbana: Univ. of Illinois Pr., 1978.

————. "*Portnoy's Complaint* (Philip Roth)." Deland, Fla.: Everett Edwards, 1973. Cassette recording.

Green, Martin. Introduction. In *A Philip Roth Reader.* New York: Farrar, 1980.

Ireland, G. W. "The Voice of Philip Roth." *Queens Quarterly* 87, no. 2 (1980): 286–92.

Jones, Judith Paterson and Guinevera A. Nance. *Philip Roth.* Modern Literature Series. New York: Ungar, 1981.

Junker, Howard. "Will This Finally Be Philip Roth's Year?" *New York,* 13 Jan. 1969, 44–47.

Kaminsky, Alice R. "Philip Roth's Professor Kepesh and the 'Reality Principle.'" *University of Denver Quarterly* 13, no. 2 (1978): 41–54.

Kliman, Bernice W. "Names in *Portnoy's Complaint.*" *Critique* 14, no. 3 (1973): 16–24.

———. "Women in Roth's Fiction." *The Nassau Review* 3, no. 4 (1978): 75–88.

Lee, Hermoine. *Philip Roth.* Contemporary Writers. New York: Methuen, 1982.

Lee, Judith Laross. "Flights of Fancy." *Chicago Review* 31, no. 4 (1980): 46–52.

Leer, Norman. "Escape and Confrontation in the Short Stories of Philip Roth." *Christian Scholar* 49, no. 2 (1966): 132–46.

McDaniel, John N. *The Fiction of Philip Roth.* Haddonfield, N.J.: Haddonfield House, 1974.

Meeter, Glenn. *Philip Roth and Bernard Malamud: A Critical Essay.* Contemporary Writers in Christian Perspective. Grand Rapids, Mich.: William B. Eerdmans, 1968.

Nelson, Gerald B. "Neil Klugman." In *Ten Versions of America.* New York: Knopf, 1972.

O'Donnell, Patrick. "The Disappearing Text: Philip Roth's *The Ghost Writer.*" *Contemporary Literature* 24, no. 3 (1983): 365–78.

Pinsker, Sanford. *The Comedy That "Hoits": An Essay on the Fiction of Philip Roth.* Literary Frontiers. Columbia: Univ. of Missouri Pr., 1975.

———. "Reading Philip Roth Reading Philip Roth." *Studies in American Jewish Literature* 3, no. 2 (1977–78); joint issue with *Yiddish* 3, no. 1 (1977): 14–18.

———. ed. *Critical Essays on Philip Roth.* Critical Essays on American Literature. Boston: G. K. Hall, 1982.

Plante, David. "Conversations with Philip: Diary of a Friendship." *The New York Times Book Review,* 1 Jan. 1984, 3, 30–31.

Raban, Jonathan. "The New Philip Roth." *Novel* 2, no. 2 (1969): 153–63.

Rodgers, Bernard F., Jr. *Philip Roth.* Twayne's United States Authors. Boston: Twayne, 1978.

Searles, George J. "Philip Roth's 'Kafka': A 'Jeu-ish American' Fiction of the First Order." *Modern Jewish Studies Annual* IV (1982); joint issue with *Yiddish* 4, no. 4 (1982): 5–11.

Siegel, Ben. "The Myths of Summer: Philip Roth's *The Great American Novel.*" *Contemporary Literature* 17, no. 2 (1976): 171–98.

Solotaroff, Theodore. "Philip Roth and the Jewish Moralists." *Chicago Review* 13, no. 1 (1959): 87–99.

Spacks, Patricia Meyer. "About Portnoy." *Yale Review* 58, no. 4 (1969): 623–35.

Tanner, Tony. "Fictionalized Recall—or 'The Settling of Scores! The Pursuit of Dreams!' (Saul Bellow, Philip Roth, Frank Conroy)." In *City of Words: American Fiction 1950–1970.* New York: Harper & Row, 1971.

Updike, John. "Yahweh Over Dionysus, in Disputed Decision." Review of *The Anatomy Lesson. The New Yorker,* 7 Nov. 1983, 174–82.

Walden, Daniel. "Goodbye, Columbus, Hello Portnoy and Beyond: The Ordeal of Philip Roth." *Studies in American Jewish Literature* 3, no. 2 (1977–78); joint issue with *Yiddish* 3, no. 1 (1977): 3–13.

Weil, Henry. "Philip Roth: Still Waiting for His Masterpiece." *Saturday Review,* June 1981, 26–31.

On John Updike

Allen, Mary. "John Updike's Love of 'Dull Bovine Beauty.'" In *The Necessary Blankness: Women in Major American Fiction of the Sixties.* Urbana: Univ. of Illinois Pr., 1976.

Atlas, James. "John Updike Breaks Out of Suburbia." *The New York Times Magazine,* 10 Dec. 1978, 60–64, 68–76.

Barnes, Jane. "John Updike: A Literary Spider." *Virginia Quarterly Review* 57, no. 1 (1981): 79–98.

Burchard, Rachael C. *John Updike: Yea Sayings.* Crosscurrents/Modern Critiques. Carbondale: Southern Illinois Univ. Pr., 1971.

Detweiler, Robert. *John Updike.* Twayne's United States Authors. New York: Twayne, 1972.

————. "John Updike and the Indictment of Culture Protestant-ism." *Four Spiritual Crises in Mid-Century American Fiction.* Univer-sity of Florida Monographs, no. 14. Gainesville: Univ. of Florida Pr., 1963.

Gado, Frank, ed. "A Conversation With John Updike." In *First Person: Conversations on Writers and Writing.* Schenectady, N.Y.: Union College Pr., 1973.

Galloway, David D. "The Absurd Man as Saint." In *The Absurd Hero in American Fiction: Updike, Styron, Bellow, Salinger.* Austin: Univ. of Texas Pr., 1966.

Gray, Paul. "Perennial Promises Kept." *Time,* 18 Oct. 1982, 72-81.

Grenier, Donald J. *The Other John Updike: Poems/Short Stories/Prose/ Play.* Athens: Ohio Univ. Pr., 1981.

Hamilton, Alice and Kenneth Hamilton. *The Elements of John Up-dike.* Grand Rapids, Mich.: William B. Eerdmans, 1970.

————. *John Updike: A Critical Essay.* Contemporary Writers in Christian Perspective. Grand Rapids, Mich.: William B. Eerd-mans, 1967.

Harper, Howard M., Jr. "John Updike: The Intrinsic Problem of Human Existence." In *Desperate Faith: A Study of Bellow, Salinger, Mailer, Baldwin, and Updike.* Chapel Hill: Univ. of North Caroli-na Pr., 1967.

Hicks, Granville. "John Updike." In *Literary Horizons.* New York: New York University, 1970.

Hill, John S. "Quest for Belief: Theme in the Novels of John Up-dike." *Southern Humanities Review* 3, no. 2 (1969): 166-78.

Howard, Jane. "Can a Nice Novelist Finish First?" *Life,* 4 Nov. 1966, 74-82.

Hunt, George. *John Updike and the Three Great Secret Things: Sex, Reli-gion, and Art.* Grand Rapids, Mich.: William B. Eerdmans, 1980.

Kakutani, Michiko. "Turning Sex and Guilt Into an American Epic." *Saturday Review,* Oct. 1981, 14-22.

Klinkowitz, Jerome. "John Updike's America." *North American Review* 265, no. 3 (1980): 68–71.

Kort, Wesley. "*The Centaur* and the Problem of Vocation." In *Shriven Selves: Religious Problems in Recent American Fiction*. Philadelphia: Fortress Press, 1972.

Lyons, Eugene. "John Updike: The Beginning and the End." *Critique* 14, no. 2 (1972): 44–59.

MacNaughton, William R., ed. *Critical Essays on John Updike*. Critical Essays on American Literature. Boston: G. K. Hall, 1982.

Markle, Joyce B. *Fighters and Lovers: Theme in the Novels of John Updike*. New York: New York Univ. Pr., 1973.

Myers, David. "The Questing Fear and Christian Allegory in John Updike's *The Centaur.*" *Twentieth Century Literature* 17, no. 2 (1971): 73–81.

Plagman, Linda A. "*Eros* and *Agape:* The Opposition in Updike's *Couples.*" *Renascence* 28, no. 2 (1976): 83–93.

Reilly, Charlie. "A Conversation With John Updike." *Canto* 3, no. 3 (1980): 148–78.

Rhode, Eric. "BBC Interview: John Updike Talks to Eric Rhode About the Shape and Subjects of His Fiction." *The Listener,* 19 June 1969, 862–64.

Samuels, Charles Thomas. "The Art of Fiction XLIII: John Updike." *Paris Review* 12, no. 45 (1968): 84–117.

————. *John Updike*. University of Minnesota Pamphlets on American Writers, no. 79. Minneapolis: Univ. of Minnesota Pr., 1969.

Schwartz, Sanford. "Top of the Class." Review of *Hugging the Shore: Essays and Criticism*. *The New York Review of Books,* 24 Nov. 1983, 26–35.

Stafford, William, and Margaret Church, eds. *Modern Fiction Studies:* John Updike Number, 20, no. 1 (1974).

Stubbs, John C. "The Search for Perfection in *Rabbit, Run.*" *Critique* 10, no. 2 (1968): 94–101.

Tanner, Tony. "A Compromised Environment (John Updike)." In *City of Words: American Fiction 1950-1970.* New York: Harper & Row, 1971.

Taylor, Larry E. *Pastoral and Anti-Pastoral Patterns in John Updike's Fiction.* Crosscurrents/Modern Critiques. Carbondale: Southern Illinois Univ. Pr., 1971.

Thomas, Lloyd Spencer. "Scarlet Sundays: Updike vs. Hawthorne." *CEA Critic* 39, no. 3 (1977): 16-17.

Thorburn, David, and Howard Eiland, eds. *John Updike: A Collection of Critical Essays.* Twentieth Century Views. Englewood Cliffs, N.J.: Prentice-Hall, 1979.

"View From the Catacombs." *Time,* 26 Apr. 1968, 66-75.

Uphaus, Suzanne Henning. *John Updike.* Modern Literature Series. New York: Frederick Ungar, 1980.

Vargo, Edward P. *Rainstorms and Fire: Ritual in the Novels of John Updike.* Port Washington, N.Y.: Kennikat, 1973.

Ward, John A. "John Updike: *The Centaur.*" *Critique* 6, no. 2 (1963): 109-14.

––––––. "John Updike's Fiction." *Critique* 5, no. 1 (1962): 27-40.

Wilhelm, Albert E. "Rabbit Restored: A Further Note on Updike's Revisions." *Notes on Modern American Literature* 6, no. 1 (1982): 7.

––––––. "Updike's Revisions of *Rabbit, Run.*" *Notes on Modern American Literature* 5, no. 3 (1981): 15.

Yates, Norris. "The Doubt and Faith of John Updike." *College English* 26, no. 4 (1965): 469-74.

Index